A CALL TO
Clarity

SET YOURSELF
free
FROM CONFUSION

JEFFREY J SHATTELL

Manufactured in the United States of America

10 9 8 7 6 5 4 3 2 1

Library of Congress Cataloging-in-Publication Data is available.

ISBN: 978-1-63769-480-0

E-ISBN: 978-1-63769-481-7

Dedication

THIS BOOK IS DEDICATED TO MY SISTER DONNA WHO IS NOW WITH JESUS

My sister Donna was full of zeal growing up. She was the second of seven children, and always seemed to be pushing the limit with most things. When she was thirty-five she became a nun. She lived a very humble life helping people in her community - very different than the somewhat wild and egocentric life she lived before. However, Donna was well educated and thoroughly enjoyed passing that knowledge on to the many children she taught. It was her favorite activity of her service.

When I turned my life over to Christ in my 30's, we started building a closer relationship. We had long, deep discussions about the Bible, family and politics, even challenging each other spiritually. I remember one fall afternoon she called me at work and said, "You need to get that book done!" She felt that I had been procrastinating the creation of this book, and she was right. She said, "I am giving you until Christmas to get that book done!" She passed away one week later. It was my mission to finish this book. Yes, I did meet her deadline. This is for you Donna! Thank you for all your wisdom, encouragement, love and humor – especially your humor.

Endorsement

I have known Jeff Shattell for more than twenty years. He has ministered in our Healing Rooms and served in our prophetic ministry with distinction. He is not only a very spiritually gifted Christian, but what I love most about Jeff is that he is 100 percent sold out for Jesus. Jeff has a burning desire to rescue those oppressed by the enemy. This book can set your mind free from the confusion that hinders you. If we are to become the overcomers Jesus has called us to be, we must renew our minds to gain clarity in all that we do. This book is highly recommended to help you find the clear path to your eternal destiny.

APOSTLE VINCENT AQUILINO

NORTH EAST REGIONAL DIRECTOR,

INTERNATIONAL ASSOCIATION OF HEALING ROOMS

Foreword

I was once asked to provide a brief summary of a forty-hour course on spiritual warfare. After a moment of thought, in which I remembered the tag line from the old *Name That Tune* television show, I responded with, "I think I can do this in ninety seconds."

The summary came through a paraphrase of John 10:10. The enemy comes to steal your peace, because he knows without peace, he can keep you bound in chaos and confusion. He comes to kill your joy, because he knows without joy you have no strength to stand against him. But ultimately, the enemy comes to destroy your testimony, because he knows without the word of your testimony you cannot overcome him by the Blood of the Lamb. But Jesus came to give you abundant life!

The enemy's diabolical work is methodical and sequential, and once he has you in the swirl of chaos and confusion, like wrestling an alligator, he quickly pulls you under the current of life and drains your strength. In *A Call to Clarity, Setting Yourself Free from Confusion* Jeff Shattell exposes the enemy's foundational efforts of using confusion to birth fear in a Believer's soul, so the enemy can hinder Believer's from attaining their density in Christ.

Discovering, exposing, and thwarting the roots of chaos

and confusion is an essential step in defeating the works of darkness associated with witchcraft and occult practitioners. This book places a tool in the Believer's spiritual warfare arsenal, enabling them to gain and maintain the freedom Jesus won for them. More importantly, understanding how to stand against confusion is essential for Believer's whom the Lord has called to be watchmen on the wall for the deliverance and inner healing of individuals, families, cities, and nations.

Understanding and implementing the principles found on the following pages will help Believers move in greater clarity toward the abundant life Jesus came to give us.

APOSTLE ALBERT E. HAUCK, PHD

PRESIDENT OF APOSTOLIC INTERCESSORS NETWORK,

A FOR PROFIT BUSINESS PROVIDING STRATEGICALLY DESIGNED INTERCESSORY TEAMS FOR LEADERS IN THE SEVEN MOUNTAINS OF CULTURE ON SIX CONTINENTS. WWW.AINCONNECT.COM

Acknowledgements

This book wouldn't be written if it wasn't for the following people that have impacted my life so greatly.

My wife Kim.

My three children Bailey, Tessa, and Jeremy.

Vincent and Deborah Aquilino

James and Peggy McLaughlin

Pastor Donald Lain

Pastor David Forsythe

Pastor Lawrence Falco

The staff at the Healing Rooms in Syracuse

Timothy Bennett – Book Preparation

Introduction

This book takes a look at confusion in a way most people have never thought of – how it affects us spiritually. Confusion affects every facet of our lives. It enters when we don't know it; it hinders when we don't see it. *A Call to Clarity* teaches us about where confusion comes from, how it afflicts us and how to gain freedom from it.

Contents

CHAPTER 1:

Where Did My Quest Begin?

One morning, during prayer in my basement, my prayer closet, I was asking the Lord some questions about MS and I needed answers. Surprisingly, God began impressing on my heart that my disease was/is tied to a "spirit of confusion." He also spoke to me that this spirit of confusion is also tied to many issues we all face today. As I continued to seek Him on the subject, he prompted me to begin a Bible study on the topic of confusion. As I dove into the Word and started writing down what the Lord was showing me, I found this spirit has persisted throughout history, almost from the beginning, and it has permeated every segment of society, including each of the Seven Mountains of society we often hear about in Christian teaching (there is a chapter devoted to this topic later in the book).

As I compiled the information the Lord was showing me, I began developing a teaching about this fascinating and pertinent piece of spiritual warfare to present to the body of Christ (2 Corinthians 2:11, "lest Satan should take

advantage of us; for we are not ignorant of his devices").
The more I studied the topic, the more I realized the vast
influence demonic confusion has had on the Body of Christ,
and the world at large. Hence, my journey into the world of
confusion deepened, and oh, what a world I found! While
I continued my research and writing, I sensed God wanted
me to share it on a broader scale, which I interpreted to
mean taking the message on the road. However, one night
He awakened me and spoke to my heart that I needed to
first write a book on the subject.

I believe one of the enemy's greatest tools is confusion, because if he can cause us to be confused about our
identity, to operate in doubt and unbelief and to be drawn
away from the truth, he can lead us away from our destiny – which is part of his plan to "to steal, and to kill, and
to destroy" (John 10:10). If he can persuade us to believe
his lies, then we won't know who we are; we won't know
who God is; we won't know our destiny or purpose in the
Kingdom; and we will miss God's voice and direction in
our lives. When we start believing the lies of the enemy, we
enable the spirit of confusion to operate. Once we choose to
believe the lie over the truth, we are in a state of confusion,
which leads us from the path of God. The enemy uses confusion in myriad places such as disease, abortion, homosexuality, witchcraft, idolatry, false religion, perversion, chaos,
addiction--even the Seven Mountains of our culture (this is
discussed in depth in a later chapter), and our salvation and
identity.

WHERE DID MY QUEST BEGIN?

Through this book, we'll discuss how the enemy comes in with confusion--what opens the door, what it is tied to, how the enemy uses it, and how to free yourself from it. We'll look at how the Word of God brings clarity and vision to dispel the confusion, and how we can walk in truth, order, purpose and understanding, rather than stumbling under the shadow of confusion.

SOMETHING TO THINK ABOUT.

Think how often the enemy lies to you on a daily basis.

Now go to the Word and write down what God says about those lies. For every lie the enemy speaks, God has the antidote in His Word. Meditate on the truth, not the lies!

CHAPTER 2

What Is Confusion?

Let's begin by looking at the meaning of confusion, so we can start on the same page, and begin to understand what the devil is trying to accomplish through this spirit. The word "confusion" (Strong's Hebrew 1101vf, balel) means "Babel, Babylonia, Babylon, to confuse, to mix, to be brought to shame, to confound, to fail to discern, to damn." It also can mean incest or perversion (Strong's 8397n, tebel). The word in Hebrew means "Babel, Babylonia or Babylon." You will see this reference often. When I first started into this study, the Lord took me on a tour through some Scriptures. Every time I saw the word Babylon, He had me replace it with the word confusion. It was a revelation that opened my eyes to see how confusion operates and how prevalent it is in this world.

One of the definitions of confusion is "shame," a far-to-prevalent weapon of the enemy we receive because we believe the lie of the enemy that we have to carry it when we fall or fail. In other words, we believe the shame belongs to us, because we don't know who we are in Christ. When our thoughts and beliefs are not aligned with God's Word, it opens a door to confusion. When we believe the lies over the truth, we become confused. Then we act on our confusion by making bad decisions, mistakes, and assumptions--all based on this lie. We don't have to receive shame--ever! It doesn't matter what we do. If we realize God is a forgiving God Who loves us no matter what, then we won't receive the shame. When we don't understand our position in Christ, we receive what the enemy says instead. That's where the confusion always comes from-- when we don't understand our relationship with God and we don't know, or don't believe, the Word of God. In this state, unfortunately, we open ourselves up to the voice of the enemy.

Confusion also means "to mix or mingle." Mixing and mingling might be good social activities, but when it comes to the Word of God, we want to steer clear of them. When you mix anything with the truth of God, you get a half-truth, which is no truth, and therefore, a lie. The lie super-sedes the truth because the two can't exist together like oil and water. Either it's a lie OR it's the truth--you can't have both. The world is full of half-truths, contorted truth, suggested truth, untruth--it's all misleading and deceptive. Most people operate out of their own subjective truth (what they feel, or think is right), but that's not truth either. The only real truth in this world is the Word of God, so everything we hear, read, and see in the world, must be lined up with that--God's Word is the plumb line.

Isaiah 5:20 says, *"Woe unto them that call evil good, and good evil; that put darkness for light, and light for darkness; that put bitter for sweet, and sweet for bitter!"* The world calls good evil and evil good. This is the epitome of confusion.

Confusion also means "incest" or "perversion." We see this consistently in our society with the non-gender movement gaining traction right now. People don't know if they are male, female, homosexual, heterosexual, bisexual or asexual. Gender confusion is extremely prevalent and loud. The Bible says in Genesis 5:2, "He created them male and female, and He blessed them and named them Man in the day when they were created." God does not make mistakes! No one is a mistake.

We are made in the image and likeness of God, exactly how God designed us. He is the perfect Creator of all mankind; He doesn't make mistakes. However, the spirit of confusion brings in a spirit of perversion, which twists and perverts the truth of God so many believe a perverted lifestyle is not only acceptable, but good. We can see how the spirit of confusion is the root of today's gender identity crisis. They are confused about who they are and about who God made them to be. And, of course, because the enemy loves to twist and pervert the Word of God, it leads people into sin instead of righteousness. As a result, they become entangled in sin as well as confusion, because we know the Word says any form of sexuality, apart from a monogamous heterosexual relationship within marriage, is sin. It's confusion that leads people into sin, which draws them away from the Lord. As Paul wrote, we know, among other things, unrepented sexual sin closes the door to Heaven, *"Or do you not know that wrongdoers will not inherit the kingdom of God? Do not be deceived: Neither the sexually immoral nor idolaters nor adulterers nor men who have sex with men..."* 1 Cor 6:9. Sexual sin is an abomination to God, and the spirit of confusion is the culprit behind the scenes.

Some other definitions of confusion (from *Webster's Dictionary*) include: "to be perplexed, to bring ruin, to be embarrassed, to disturb in mind or purpose, to blur, to bring disorder or to mix up." Also, "to have incertitude, unsureness, doubt, ignorance, disorganization, untidiness, chaos, or mayhem."

"Confound" is another synonym of confusion the enemy employs, but it also means, "to damn or curse something or someone." So, not only does confusion prevent us from knowing the truth, it also can bring a curse that could prevent us from being able to understand it. Many people already live in confusion because they don't know the truth, but now they *can't* know the truth, because they can't understand the Gospel, even when they read it or hear it. Are you beginning to see how the enemy works through this spirit? It's a devious spirit that can permeate every area of our lives. It is one of the most effective tools that enables the enemy to bring ruin and thwart destinies.

WHAT IS CONFUSION?

Another weapon the enemy uses through confusion is lack of discernment. When we operate in confusion, we lack the discernment needed from the Holy Spirit. The Holy Spirit will speak to us at times guiding and directing us through situations and events. However, when confusion is involved, discernment is dulled, and mistakes are made. People make decisions and have perceptions that are incorrect because they aren't walking in truth. It's so important to live in truth and allow the Holy Spirit to be sharp in us, so that in every situation, we are able to hear His voice and act in line with the Lord.

I am reminded of a time I walked up to a drive-through ATM. A van pulled up about ten feet from me and asked for directions. I answered the driver and he said he couldn't hear me. As I started stepping closer to the van so he could hear what I was saying, my Holy Spirit discernment alarm went off. I instantly sensed I needed to get away fast. Just then, the side door of the van popped open, and I could see two men getting ready to jump out. I knew they were going to grab me, so I immediately moved away, and they sped off. Thank God for discernment! We need God's discernment in all areas of our lives, and at all times. It's so important to stay in truth and, thereby, to properly discern the leading of God.

To fulfill our destiny, we need clarity. Earlier, I mentioned that one of the meanings of confusion (in the Hebrew) was "Babylon." Babylon means "gate of the gods" in the Greek. Note the correlation between the two: con-

A CALL TO CLARITY

ᴸe door (gate) to the enemy who wants us to
ᴸf who we are and who we represent. The Bible
. *Rev 18:2, 3, "...Babylon (confusion) is a dwelling
ᴸce for demons, a prison for foul spirits, and a cage for
the unclean." Putting the word confusion in place of Babylon here paints an ugly picture of what confusion looks
like. People who suffer from confusion are often tormented

to the extreme, because it causes such an identity crisis—a
kind of spiritual schizophrenia, if you will. Unfortunately,
the devil thrives there.

SOMETHING TO THINK ABOUT.

Meditate on all the different definitions of confusion
you just read about, and think about how they affect you
and your life.

CHAPTER 3

History of Confusion/ Babylon

As we continue, let's look at the history of Babylon (keep in mind Babylon means confusion), which was birthed at the same time as the Tower of Babel. As the following verses describe, the people of this city were prideful and seeking their own glory as opposed to seeking the glory of God.

In Genesis 11:1-4, 7: *"Now the whole world had one language and a common speech.... They said to each other, 'Come, let's make bricks and bake them thoroughly.' They used brick instead of stone, and tar for mortar. Then they said, 'Come, let us build ourselves a city, with a tower that reaches to the heavens, so that we may make a name for ourselves; otherwise, we will be scattered over the face of the whole earth.' But the Lord came down to see the city*

*and the tower the people were building. The Lord said,
'If as one people speaking the same language, they have
begun to do this, then nothing they plan to do will be impossible for them. Come, let us go down and confuse their
language so they will not understand each other.'"*

*7 "So the Lord scattered them from there over all the
earth, and they stopped building the city. That is why it was
called Babel--because there the Lord confused the language of the whole world. From there the Lord scattered
them over the face of the whole earth."*

The Babylonians thought they could make their own
way to Heaven without God. They didn't call on Him for
help or to ask for instruction, or even dedicate the tower to
Him. They didn't think they needed God. God, therefore,
had to intervene to demonstrate to them who He was.

Babylon was known for witchcraft and divination.
Virtually all pagan practices began in the city of Babylon
during the time of Nimrod. Since then, those pagan practices have wormed there way into almost every religion. The
Tower of Babel was actually tied to Satan worship with the
use of fire, the sun, and the serpent. The Babylonians had
more than a hundred gods. Some of the major ones were:
Adapa (god of wisdom), Irra (god of plagues), Ishtar (goddess of passion, prostitution, and war) and where we get the
word Easter), Marduk (god of magic), Nabu (god of writing
and wisdom), and Zaltu (goddess of strife). There were also
gods of plagues of sickness and disease.

HISTORY OF CONFUSION/BABYLON

We see the results of the influence of these gods on our culture in myriad ways. We, as a nation, are consumed with perversion and sex, which permeates everything we watch on a daily basis. Additionally, we have a culture that is obsessed with the occult – psychics, vampires, witches, drugs, etc. The god of magic has been busy entertaining the spirit of witchcraft, and we're more than happy to participate. Thanks to the god Nabu, we are also obsessed with intellectualism. Secular humanism is a common way of thinking in the world today. There are so many people think they don't need God. They prefer to rely on their own mind, philosophical beliefs, and experiences. They believe they are bigger than God. This intellectual way of thinking has also infiltrated our culture--compliments of Greek culture. The Greek mindset has saturated our education system and has effectively replaced the Word of God in the classroom.

We also can see the goddess of strife operating in this country as well. Look at the hostility and division we are seeing in people groups right now. And, of course, we see sickness and disease at every turn. All of these spirits are operating throughout society--including the church. Let's look at some of the doors that give them entrance into our lives.

SOMETHING TO THINK ABOUT.

Read the story of the Tower of Babel in Genesis 11. Study it and understand how it could overlap in today's world and in our lives.

Look at the definitions of confusion and be alert if you see them operating in your sphere of influence. Deal with them appropriately.

CHAPTER 4

Open Doors

First and foremost, we need to understand if we are born-again believers in Jesus Christ- and have invited Jesus into our hearts and lives, asked Him to forgive us of our sins, and are walking in righteousness-we have nothing to worry about. We just need to take authority over the enemy to receive our freedom. However, in many cases, we have opened the door, which has allowed the enemy to afflict us.

One thing you need to understand is the devil is a legal-ist. The kingdom of darkness is a legal entity, much like the Kingdom of Light is a legal entity. God has a government with rules and consequences, and so does the devil. When we sin, we give the devil a legal right to afflict us. He goes running to God and accuses us of whatever we did, and God must accept it according to His Word. Now, I can hear all of you out there saying, "But the Blood of Jesus! The Blood of Jesus!" And yes, the Blood of Jesus does cover our sins. However, what many believers don't understand is sin must be repented of FIRST! Through repentance and believing Jesus died on the Cross for our sins, His Blood atones for our sin, which releases us from the legal trap into which we've been snared.

However, it is essential we understand how we gave legal ground to the enemy and how we allowed him to oppress us. We need to ask ourselves: What did we say, or what did we do, to open the door to the enemy? We also need to ask for personal revelation about our specific situation. That is the key to removing the enemy's confusion and walking in truth and clarity. Once we know where it came in, then we can repent and close the door.

Open doors are areas in our lives where we have compromised the Word and entered into sin. Sin is a choice and God gives us free will. God will warn us, but sometimes we just don't listen, and we sin anyway, which opens a door to the enemy. A door is exactly that; it's a place where the enemy is free to come and go. It gives the devil access to us, just like a door gives access to a room or building. By repenting of our sin and putting our faith in the Blood of Jesus we are, in essence, locking the door so the enemy no longer has access to cause havoc.

If we abide by the Word of God, we are safe, but when we choose to leave the Lord's protective covering by moving into sin, we inevitably suffer the consequences. To be clear, the enemy only afflicts, or oppresses, believers. Believers are not possessed by the enemy--only oppressed. He cannot possess a born-again believer, but he can certainly oppress them. We need to be quick to repent when we sin in order to shut the door as quickly as possible.

In his popular devotional, "Utmost for His Highest," Oswald Chambers exhorts readers to "quickly agree with your adversary," meaning 'fess up! Tell the Lord you know you sinned, repent for it, and ask for forgiveness. Notice Chambers says to do it "quickly," because he knows the enemy will come in if you don't.

Let's take a look at some of the doors that make us susceptible to confusion:

OPEN DOOR NUMBER 1

PRIDE, REBELLION AND IDOL WORSHIP

Genesis 11:2 - Tower of Babel

"And they said, 'Come, let us build ourselves a city, and a tower whose top is in the heavens; let us make a name for ourselves, lest we be scattered abroad over the face of the whole earth.'"

The Babylonians declared they would build their own city, eliminating God completely, and make a name for themselves. They weren't interested in glorifying God; they had their own agenda and had decided they didn't need God in order to accomplish it. They wanted to make a name for themselves.

How many times in life do we, as believers, eliminate God from our plans? How often do we make important decisions and embark on major projects and don't even consult Him? We need God involved in every part of our lives. When we don't seek Him in our daily lives for our projects

ns, we are telling Him that we know more than
nd can do a better job without Him.

We all know that's not true, but sometimes we have
momentary amnesia and make bad decisions without con-
sulting God. The problem is when we make choices without
the Lord's involvement, we open ourselves up to confusion,
because we have not used truth and wisdom in making those
choices. When we forgo truth, we welcome confusion.

Babel was the first place in the Bible where confusion
came in because of the pride and willful disobedience of the
people. God confused their language by allowing a spirit of
confusion to thwart their plans. However, He did so because
the people were in rebellion and believed they didn't need
God. They rejected God and made their own plans. They
decided they didn't need God--that they could be their own
god. And so, a spirit of confusion entered the world.

We must make sure, on a regular basis, we are not plac-
ing our own wants and plans above those of the Lord's. We
must continually seek God and follow Him, so we avoid
the consequence of confusion.

OPEN DOOR NUMBER 2

DISOBEDIENCE/UNREPENTANCE

The people of Judah wouldn't listen. Jeremiah 25:4-7:
"And the Lord has sent to you all His servants the prophets,

rising early and sending them, but you have not listened nor inclined your ear to hear. *⁵ They said, 'Repent now everyone of his evil way and his evil doings, and dwell in the land that the Lord has given to you and your fathers forever and ever. ⁶ Do not go after other gods to serve them and worship them, and do not provoke Me to anger with the works of your hands; and I will not harm you. Yet you have not listened to Me,' says the Lord, 'that you might provoke Me to anger with the works of your hands to your own hurt.'"*

In other words, Jeremiah is saying, "God sent you clear instructions and you have not listened." The verse before this says God has called you to change your ways for twenty-three years, but to no avail. There was also an unwillingness to repent among the people. Once they were called out by God for their disobedience, they needed to repent. There was idol worship. This seems to be a common theme. What is separating us from God? Do we have idols such as: money, people, job, success, the list goes on and on? We need to repent of whatever has taken God's place. God is saying be quick to repent, quick to obey, and quick to get rid of any idols!

The people of Judah were sent to Babylon (confusion) for seventy years because of this. Remember, the devil is a legalist. If we are disobedient, or refuse to repent, or have idols in our lives, the enemy has legal ground to bring confusion. In this instance, it meant seven decades of bondage! We have Jesus, so let's repent and live in freedom! Slam the door to the enemy!

A CALL TO CLARITY

OPEN DOOR NUMBER 3

SPIRIT OF RELIGION/CONTROL

This next story in the Word tells of a man named Passhur who wanted to stop the Word of God from coming forth. The spirit of religion and the spirit of control want to stop the anointed of God from speaking His Word. Sadly, many times in the church, this is due to competition among church leaders. There is a lot to this story so please pay attention. Here we go:

- *Jeremiah 20:2 – *"Then Pashhur struck Jeremiah the prophet and put him in the stocks that were in the high gate of Benjamin, which was* by the house of the Lord.

- *3 And it happened on the next day that Pashhur brought Jeremiah out of the stocks. Then Jeremiah said to him, 'The Lord has not called your name Pashhur, but Magor-Missabib.*

- *4 'For thus says the Lord: 'Behold, I will make you a terror to yourself and to all your friends; and they shall fall by the sword of their enemies, and your eyes shall see it.* I will give all Judah into the hand of the king of Babylon, and he shall carry them captive to Babylon and slay them with the sword.

- *5 'Moreover I will deliver all the wealth of this city, all its produce, and all its precious things; all the treasures of the kings of Judah I will give into the*

34

hand of their enemies, who will plunder them, seize them, and carry them to Babylon.

- *⁶'And you, Pashhur, and all who dwell in your house, shall go into captivity. You shall go to Babylon, and there you shall die, and be buried there, you and all your friends, to whom you have prophesied lies.'"*

Pashhur was in charge of keeping order in the temple. He was the temple's overseer. He decided to lock up Jeremiah, God's anointed man for Israel. But there were consequences for stopping the Word from going forth and it opens a door.

Notice God changed his name from Pashhur to Magor-Missabib. Pashhur means freedom, Magor-Missabib means fear on every side. Think about this freedom to fear. God says in verse 4, he would have terror on every side. It also says in verse 5 he will live in poverty! It also affects others. Verse 6 says you and all your household will be in bondage in Babylon (confusion). Then God's Word even mentions his friends. He chose to try and stop the Word from going forth and now he was going to a place of fear! The spirit of religion and control locks up the Word of God. God sent him to a land of confusion (Babylon)! If we feel we have a spirit of religion or control in us or others, we need to deal with it. If we have ever stopped the Word of God or tried to stop an anointed person of God from moving in their calling, we need to repent. Don't forget this will affect others too--hurting family, friends and our loved ones. We cannot allow the enemy to use this to bring confusion into our lives. The enemy loves it when we open doors, and he will gladly walk through. This can be the reason many people leave their churches or start their own—maybe even leading to new denominations. They are stopped from moving in their giftings by religious and controlling spirits so they must go elsewhere to fulfill their callings. Even worse they never move in ministry again because they feel they have nothing to offer. My wife and I have seen this firsthand. Jesus made it very easy for all of us. He said, "follow Me!" He didn't say follow the teachings of the Methodists, the Lutherans, or the Pentecostals. He said follow Me! Guess what that means? Follow His whole word because the Word (Jesus) was made flesh. Simple! Do you think there is a little confusion going on here? The enemy loves this.

Do you struggle with your finances? This may be the cause. This same spirit can affect your finances. It is legal ground for the enemy.

Do you struggle with fear and terror? Same situation. Is it possible that you have allowed the enemy in by this way?

God wants unity and oneness in His church! Let's repent and follow the King! Speak life into God's people rather than death. When we speak negatively, or try to hold back His people, we are opening a door wide to the enemy and derailing a destiny at the same time. Repent! Shut the door! Let's get out of the land of confusion!

OPEN DOOR NUMBER 4

ENVY AND SELF-SEEKING

James 3:16 - *For where envy and self-seeking exist, confusion and every evil thing are there.*

Do we have envy in our lives? It is very easy to walk in this. The word "envy" translates to jealousy. Have you ever been jealous? This can apply to so many areas of our lives. We may think *I wish I could have a family like theirs; their children are so good. I wish my husband made as much money as her husband. Then we would not have all these financial problems. My wife isn't as pretty as his wife.* How about this one? *I wish I were as anointed as she/he is. Her voice is amazing.* Or *How come God speaks to them so clearly and not me? Why am I struggling with this sickness when that person over there seems to be always healthy and they aren't even walking with God!* What are you jealous about? What are you self-seeking about? We all need to ask ourselves these questions because it opens a big door for the enemy to come rushing through. The Bible says later in this verse *confusion and every evil thing* will be there! When we start walking in jealousy, we are sending an open invitation to the enemy and his cohorts to come and party. He gladly brings his confusion and every evil thing. That's right—the Word says *every evil thing*! Just think of that for a minute. When we open this door, we are allowing the legalist enemy to bring in every evil thing into our lives.

As we mentioned before, God will not go against His

' admit, I do get frustrated when I hear Chris-
things and grumbling. Thankfulness is a
₀o counter these attitudes. Do we really under-
₋d and believe we are going to Heaven? We need to keep
our focus on Jesus and look at life on this Earth as an opportunity to share what God has given us. The greatest gift,
the gospel message, needs to be shared with others. I have
said for a long time our time on Earth is like a fourteen second pit stop. Eternity is forever. The trials we go through
here are but a second in the grand scheme of things. We
will spend eternity in a glorious place called Heaven. We
have something glorious to share. His Name is Jesus! The
Lord spoke to me one morning and He said, "Boy, you have
quite the list every morning! When was the last time you
asked, 'What can I do for you today, Lord?'" That really
got my attention. Please don't misunderstand what God was
asking me. He wasn't saying He didn't want to bless me, or
He wasn't saying He didn't want to answer my prayers. He
was simply saying, *Jeff you are self-seeking. It is always
about you and your circle of influence.* He was saying, *Seek
me first and all of those things will follow.*

He also spoke to me about what was/is going on with a
lot of Christians. He said, *Many people seek the blessing or
a miracle more than My presence.* Ouch! I know I have been
guilty of this in the past. I remember sowing seed for a blessing, but was I doing it just to get something? I am not saying,
don't sow a seed, I am saying, always seek His presence first
and the blessing will follow. It is a heart issue!

As I wrote earlier, I have been diagnosed with a nasty neurological disease. I sensed God asking me: *Would you take your healing over My Presence?* Brutal question. I want to make this very clear. God wasn't saying I don't want to heal you or it's either your healing or Me. What He was really saying was: *Are you so focused on the miracle you are looking right past Me?* Now, of course, we know what the right answer is. I used to be very physically active, and I loved playing sports and working with my hands. I enjoyed physical labor, loved the outdoors with my three kids, and just loved life and then…it happened. After fifty years of perfect health—BAM! I might have gotten a stuffy nose every five years. Other than that, I had no health issues. It started with numbness in my legs and arms, and it has progressed to the point now where I can barely walk, barely write my name, and I still need to provide for my family. I was shocked to hear the doctor say they couldn't help me. Seven doctors and seven lousy reports. Let me tell you, I want to be healed! I also believe by His stripes I have been healed.

That being said, He also spoke to my spirit *With My Presence comes the blessing.* So, no matter what goes on in the natural, all I need to do is seek His Presence. The healing will come. The moral of this story is when we chase after the blessing/miracles we very often look past His Presence. What are God's priorities for us? Jesus tells us in His Word to "Seek first the Kingdom of God." Remember the miracles followed the disciples. He wants us to leave a trail of His Presence everywhere we go.

', we need to stay away from envy, jealou-

ʒ. We need to repent and shut this barn

OPEN DOOR NUMBER 5

SEXUAL SIN/PERVERSION

Leviticus 18 talks about sexual sin. God calls it perversion, which is the same word as confusion. We all have a past, and we all fall short of the glory of God. That being said, we need to be sure we deal with every sexual sin in our lives. Jesus even said if we think of these things in our heart, we have committed them. We need to stay as pure as we possibly can, believing what is impossible for man is possible with God. Do not be enticed by the enemy. Stand strong with the King and His Word! The enemy is constantly looking for an opening. God knows your weaknesses, but guess what? So does the enemy. He is watching you. He reminds us of that ex-boyfriend or that pretty co-worker and maybe even arranges 'random' meetings with them. He wants us to get to the internet, and not for a Bible study. He wants to bring confusion into our marriages, our relationships. During the hard times in a marriage, we can get bombarded with doubts—*Why didn't I marry that girl from high school? That man at work is nice and is giving me a lot of attention I don't get at home.* Confusion brings doubt, brings division. It undermines relationships! It will divide families and break up marriages. And it can weasel its way into our children's lives.

My wife and I have done a lot of personal ministry. Some of the worst cases are usually someone that has been sexually assaulted. Male or female, it doesn't matter. It very often brings in major confusion, depression, unworthiness, and it wasn't even their fault. I believe it is very important to break all these possible effects off its victims. Unfortunately, these people often have identity issues, substance abuse issues, and mental and emotional disorders. The spirit of confusion is there when this trauma happens and is waiting at the door to harass them. It can go on for as long as they stay unsaved and beyond. Sometimes it takes another Christian to see objectively when a person is being oppressed by confusion.

We need to deal with sexual sin/perversion in our lives today. Repent and slam the door shut to this foul spirit. Remember Jesus always has His arms wide open. Jesus heals!

OPEN DOOR NUMBER 6

SHAME

Psalm 40:15 (NKJV)

"Let them be confounded because of their shame."

The Lord is saying here that through our own shame we have opened the door to confusion. The word "shame" here means shameful thing. This is not pertaining to the shame the enemy tries to put on us. This is shame we put on ourselves, usually through sin. Shame can come in many different forms. Sometimes, people will try to bring shame on us. I have seen this many times in ministry. People may say, "Grandpa died because of the way you (the caretaker) took care of him." In fact, you may have done your very best with grandpa. This type of shame is very common. People often say things like: "We lost the game because of you." or "We didn't hit our financial goal at the office because of you." This attack of the enemy is what is called in Scripture as the "accusing of the brethren." If we take these darts of the enemy to heart it can be very damaging to our relationship with God and others.

The way I try to look at shame is being aware of the conviction of the Holy Spirit. If He convicts me of something, I need to repent. Another question to ask is: Would Jesus approve of these actions? If not, we are doing a shameful act and need to repent quickly. Jesus makes this simple. We confess our sin to Him and believe He cleanses us of it by faith in His shed Blood at the Cross. Of course, we need to be ready for accusations of the enemy who will want us to stay in condemnation for all the shameful acts we've done and try to bring false shame on us, making us think we are not forgiven. Don't be deceived by the devil, he is always looking for an opening. If you do something that doesn't honor God, repent and move on. Do not allow the legalist to come and bring confusion!

OPEN DOORS TO CONFUSION

OPEN DOOR NUMBER 7

BROKEN COVENANTS

We are going to look at a story in 2 Chronicles 36:11. Zedekiah made an oath to King Nebuchadnezzar by God.

- 2 Chronicles 36:11 - *Zedekiah was twenty-one years old when he became king, and he reigned eleven years in Jerusalem.*

- 12 *He did evil in the sight of the Lord his God, and did not humble himself before Jeremiah the prophet, who spoke from the mouth of the Lord.*

- 13 *And he also rebelled against King Nebuchadnezzar, who had made him swear an oath by God; but he stiffened his neck and hardened his heart against turning to the Lord God of Israel.*

This word "oath" means fidelity to a lord, the obligation, or the engagement to be faithful to a lord, or in this instance King Nebuchadnezzar. He swore this by God. In other words, He tied God to this. But he didn't stand by his word. Very interesting Zedekiah's name means "the Lord is just." God doesn't go against His Word, and He expects us to keep ours! Let's look at the consequences of Zedekiah's actions. Ezekiel 17:19, 20 refers to this.

- 19 *"Therefore thus says the Lord God: 'As I live, surely My oath which he despised, and My covenant which he broke, I will recompense on his own* head. *20 I will spread My net over him, and he shall be taken in My snare. I will bring him to Babylon and try him there for the treason which he committed against Me.'"*

When Zedekiah broke his oath to King Nebuchadnezzar God refers to it as "treason" in His Word. Think about the word treason. That is a really tough word. He is saying when we break an oath under God, we are committing treason against God Himself! Look at the meanings.

- Treason - the crime of betraying one's country, especially by attempting to kill the sovereign or overthrowing the government.

- Treachery - disloyalty, betrayal, faithlessness, mutiny, rebellion

God is saying when we break an oath, we are betraying His country (Kingdom). Think about that. In God's eyes, when we break an oath, we are betraying Him. Ouch! He says it is disloyal. Do we want to be disloyal to Him? If I were to ask you, "Will you commit mutiny against God with me?" I would hope everyone's answer would be "No. Of course not!" It breaks my heart thinking about this. How many times in our lives have we committed treason against God?

So, what was God's punishment against Zedekiah for this act? God sent him to Babylon (confusion). To the land of confusion! How many oaths have you broken in the past? Divorce is rampant in our country, even among Christians. But wasn't the marriage vow an oath, a broken covenant?! Have you ever broken a contract? I know I have. In the workplace, how far does this go? Does this principle apply when we make a verbal oath or commitment? It used to be "my word is my bond" and a handshake was all that was necessary to seal the deal. Does this mandate of God apply to situations where we tell someone we will be somewhere and then we don't show up? It's an interesting concept, isn't it? What about not going to a doctor's appointment when we agreed to be there? How about this scenario: you told your neighbor you would water their plants, or take out their dog, but you didn't follow through? Yet, you verbally gave them your word.

Case in point. My wife and I had made a pledge to a building fund at a church we were attending a long time ago. We felt the Lord saying our season at this church was over, so we left. We just figured since He allowed us to leave, and we were no longer going to the church we no longer had to give to the building fund. Surprise. Surprise. Six months later the Lord convicted us of our commitment, and I ended up meeting with a church leader and getting the balance we owed so we could square up. I honestly believe if we didn't make it right with our obligation to that church, it would have been an open door for the enemy to bring in confusion. Has this ever happened to you? Have you ever made a commitment like this and not followed through? How about defaulting on a loan? Remember, the devil is a legalist. Don't give him an opportunity to bring in confusion. Repent and make things right, if possible, and shut the door to the enemy.

A CALL TO CLARITY

The Bible instructs us to let our "yes" be "yes" and our "no" be "no." We need to be people of our word. When we say something, or make an oath or contract, we need to stand by it, regardless of the cost or circumstances.

Now that we see the open doors the enemy uses to get into our lives, let's see how it can affect us.

SOMETHING TO THINK ABOUT.

What are the most common open doors?

Take a good look at our own life. Do you need to shut some doors to the enemy?

CHAPTER 5

Results of Confusion in Our Lives

1. SICKNESS AND DISEASE

This is where it all started with me. I was diagnosed with an autoimmune disease. The doctors don't know how to cure it and they gave me very little hope. It started with a numbness on my right side while I was playing in a basketball tournament. I loved being active, playing ball, hiking, and playing with my kids almost every day in the backyard. We were always playing. I also had a very physical job and I loved it.

After that basketball tournament, I tripped on a stick that was only half an inch off the ground while hiking in the Adirondacks with my kids. I decided I better see a doctor. The first physician couldn't find anything wrong. He sent me to a neurologist. It then took this specialist a number of MRIs to find the problem. He said I had an autoimmune disease and there was no cure. He also said several negative things like: "You will be in a wheelchair and you will never be the same!"

I started to do some research. I discovered autoimmune diseases affect 20% of the population in the United States alone, which means 50 million people are affected. That really got my attention. *Can you believe this*? I thought to myself. There must be something to this. It seemed like so many people I knew were suffering with some type of auto-immune disorder. What was the common thread? What was the root? There are over one hundred autoimmune diseas-es. One hundred! This is what I found in a medical report I found on the internet about them, "It's unknown what causes the confusion within the immune system. There are numerous theories as to what causes autoimmune diseases, but no concrete evidence. "

See more at: **http://www.bandbacktogether.com/auto-immune-disorders-resources/#sthash.KC9eGmAb.dpuf**

"It's unknown what causes the confusion within the im-mune system." Really? Confusion causes us so much grief and now confusion attacks our bodies also? This really hit me like a two by four over the head! The Lord was so clear to me when I read this. He really highlighted the word "confusion." Now I knew confusion was very often tied to people into the occult, but I never thought it could be tied to something like this. He said it is the "spirit of confusion" that causes much of this.

RESULTS OF CONFUSION IN OUR LIVES

It makes so much sense. Think about how s͏ʳ
immune system is acting when they suffer witi͏.
sclerosis (MS). The doctors say the person's good im͏...
cells attack their very own myelin sheath. In other words,
the body attacks itself. It destroys perfectly good cells.
Does this sound right? Does this sound like something God
would design? Even the doctors are baffled by this action.
In my case, my immune system operated to perfection my
whole life up to that point. I would go years without even
getting a cold and we had three kids always bringing home
whatever was the sickness of the week from school. My
work involved interacting with many people on a daily basis and I rarely got sick. What could be the problem? When
I saw this, it finally made sense.

I discovered the way these autoimmune diseases are often treated is by suppressing the immune system. They give
all types of drugs, even some chemotherapy medications.
Rather than focusing on why the immune system is confused, the medical community treats these diseases by suppressing the whole immune system, which makes patients
more susceptible to other sickness and diseases. Why don't
we just find out what causes this rather than focusing on the
symptoms? Please don't take what I am saying as an excuse
not to go to a doctor. That is not what I am saying. What I
am saying is we need to go to God first, then deal with the
spiritual in conjunction with the doctors, not excluding the
input of medical practitioners. I feel you will find that there
is always victory in God's word.

Here are just a few of the auto immune diseases.

- Arthritis

- Celiac disease – can't eat gluten, or it will damage the small intestine.

- Crohn's disease – immune system attacks the lining of the intestine.

- Grave's disease – the immune system produces antibodies overstimulate the thyroid gland, which causes the disease.

- Colitis - immune system attacks the lining of the intestine.

- Type 1 diabetes – immune system produces antibodies that attack insulin-producing cells in the pancreas.

- Rheumatoid arthritis – The immune system produces antibodies that attach to the linings of the joints. The immune system then attacks the joints causing inflammation.

- Multiple sclerosis (MS) – Immune system attacks nerve cells.

- Psoriasis – overactive immune system which causes skin irritation.

As you can see, the immune system is attacking good cells. It is confused. This doesn't make sense. The immune system is supposed to attack organisms that invade the body. The immune system is a combination of cells, tissues and organs that protect the body. The system is obviously confused. God is not the author of confusion. He designs perfection. We need to deal with this confusion.

We have to break confusion off of our bodies! We need to tell our cells to act the way they were designed. Take the authority God has given you. First, however, we need to find the open door, or doors. Remember we went over them. Kick confusion out and slam the door shut. Speak healing over yourself. By His stripes you have been healed! Victory is yours!

2. CONFUSION AND ABORTION

Abortion is one of saddest things this world has embraced by a long shot. It has become what defines elections and it has become a hot button for many people. In fact, some people have become violent in regard to abortion on both sides of the controversy. But how did our society get to this point of destroying our most vulnerable members?

Our view on human life has been watered down by the enemy. We have become calloused to abortion and the taking of innocent life. In fact, the practice of killing children as been around for centuries. Child sacrifice was warned about in Leviticus 18, 20, Deuteronomy 12 and 18. The Babylonian seal had a picture representing people bringing their children to sacrifice to a god who resembles

(or Baal) having horns and sitting on a throne. The
alks about how people used to sacrifice their children
)lech.

Think of what an open door this is? Babylon took their
own children to sacrifice to some false god. How can a
person destroy their very own child? Do you see how this
spirit could be operating today with abortion? This is flat out
unnatural, and the enemy uses the fact the baby is still in the
mother's womb to convince us it is okay. Remember the devil is a legalist and he just needs an open door. He will skew
your vision of what is right. Confusion will come in and have
you thinking just the opposite of what is natural.

I remember watching TV in the early '70s and there
was an outdoor show on, and the animal expert would say
we can't tag that animal because the momma bear is right
there, and she will attack us. It's natural to protect your
young. I remember when my oldest daughter was playing
soccer in high school and she was hit maliciously by an op-
posing player to take her out of the game. It worked and the
opponent from the other team was thrown out of the game
with a red card. It really got me wound up. Even our thir-
teen-year veteran coach said she had never seen anything
like it. I was so angry, and the old pre-Jesus Jeff was looking for someone to yell at or punch (sorry). Remember I am
a diesel mechanic, and I am sometimes a little rough around
the edges. My beautiful wife, on the other hand, charac-
teristically, had everything under control and was staying
calm and composed. The coach called us over to the bench

and said we should take her to the hospital to have he
looked at. My daughter didn't want to leave, however,
the game was over and so we sat on the bench with her.

Wouldn't you know my sweet and very calm wife saw
another one of our players get shoved like our daughter
and she lost it. That was it, Miss Prim and Proper started
screaming at their whole team and at their coach. In fact,
we had to calm her down. They had stirred up the momma
bear and they better look out. I had never seen my wife ever
act like that. She was on the warpath.

The Lord reminded me of this story when I started to
look at abortion and the connection to confusion. How my
wife acted that day was totally natural. God has wired us
to protect our children. When we allow confusion into our
lives it skews our view on what is natural and right.

- Abortion clinics tell their clients that: *Transient
  feelings of guilt, sadness, or loss are common, but
  most women can overcome negative feelings that
  might affect them. It is normal to feel emotional after an abortion. While you may experience sadness
  or grief, these feelings usually go away after a few
  days.*

They tell them of the guilt and the shame that can come
from this action. Think about this, it is because it goes
against the way God wired women. He has wired them to
protect their child. Think of the women have had an abortion and suffer with guilt and shame. It says "most" women

53

can overcome this. What about the rest? They say you may feel grief and sadness. Why? Because it goes against our natural makeup. They say those feelings "usually" go away after a few days. What happens when they don't? The devil doesn't play fair and wants to burden women (and men) the rest of their days with guilt, shame, sadness, grief and depression. So sad! This confusion is one nasty spirit.

Abortion is so unnatural; it breaks my heart. Think about households where children are abused and neglected. Growing up the youngest of seven children I saw my parents sacrifice everything for us kids. We didn't have much in the line of material things, but we always had a hot meal. It is just plain normal to provide and protect your children. If you don't feel that way, you are deceived, and I think you need to deal with some confusion in your life.

I want you to know if you have had an abortion, you are not alone. In fact, almost 25% of women in the U.S. have had one by the age of 45 (jaw-dropping statistic). The fact is, though, you do not have to stay in a place of guilt, shame, and torment. Freedom starts by recognizing you are a sinner (Romans 3:23?), confessing your sins, turning away from them by repentance, and asking Jesus into your heart. He will forgive you and help you deal with the confusion in your life. (Maybe put ministries and their websites that people can check out) Find the open door and repent. Shut it completely to the enemy. I am not writing this to bring guilt, but to highlight the reasons these things may have happened. We need to deal with these things so we can truly walk out our destiny in Christ.

3. CONFUSION AND THE IDENTITY CRISIS

Who are you? Really, who are you? How would you answer that question? I could say: I am the youngest of seven. I have a wife and three children. I do this for a living and so on. The world identifies you one way, and the Bible identifies you another way.

If you don't know who God made you to be and who you represent on this Earth, you will always be searching. You will always be wondering, *What is my purpose? Why am I here?* Confusion steals our identity!

God says you are made in His image. You have His DNA in you! He doesn't make mistakes. He says in John 1:12 those who have received Jesus into their heart are now called His children. Think about that. After coming to Christ, you and I are part of the family of God, the Creator of the universe. Do you think being a child of the King may have some perks? Colossians 2:10 tells us we are "complete in Christ." The word "complete" in that verse means you are made full. So, the Creator of Heaven and Earth has made us full in Christ. We are lacking nothing. The Bible also says in Romans 8 the same Spirit raised Jesus from the dead dwells in us who believe in Him. Are you kidding me? You mean, the same Spirit raised Jesus out of the grave lives in me? If that is so, how is it possible that the enemy brings doubt? How does he get me to forget who I am and Who I represent? He brings in confusion, that's how. The Bible says to lay hands on the sick and they will recover. We need to pray in faith this will happen. The Bible says all we need is faith the size of a mustard seed and we will be able to move those mountains in our lives.

If you are second-guessing your identity in Christ, you need to deal with confusion in your life. Knowing who you are in Christ is key to the Kingdom of God. If you are walking around all day with no direction and not understanding your authority over the enemy, you will become his punching bag.

When my children were very young, my wife would often take a stand against the enemy. I remember the kids getting sick when they were very little and she flat out told the enemy, "You are not going to bring sickness against my kids in Jesus's Name!" She took the authority Jesus had given her. He says we will have "all authority" over the enemy. Not some, not once in a while, ALL! I don't think my kids missed two days of school the next thirteen years. She knew her identity, and she exercised it.

I exercised my authority in an unusual way one time when I was coming home with my son after picking him up at his college. We had been on the road for hours and we still had five hours to go to get home when a huge thunderstorm rolled in. It was raining so hard the car was hydroplaning, which slowed us down drastically. It was a huge storm, and it was raining in every direction. We really wanted to get home but, at the speed we were driving, it would take us another eight hours, instead of another five. There was no way I wanted to be home that late, so I prayed and took authority over the rain in Jesus's Name.

RESULTS OF CONFUSION IN OUR LIVES

The Bible says we will do greater things than what Jesus did in His Name. He rose people from the dead, healed, calmed storms, and the list goes on. I told the rain, "Stop now, in the Name of Jesus!" Guess what? It stopped.

The weird thing was, I could see the rain in front of our car, but it was no longer raining on our car! Crazy, huh? It still wasn't helping our hydroplaning issue, however. The road was still very wet, and the puddles were deep, so the car was still sliding dangerously. I told the roads to, "Dry up in Jesus's Name!" Guess what? They did. We could see it was still raining in the opposite lane and people still had their wipers working, but we were driving on dry, rain-free roads. God just wants us to understand who we are in Christ. What our identity is and Who we represent. The devil wants us to forget all of that and bring in despair and doubt. Deal with confusion and understand who you are in Christ!

When I was very young, I remember comparing my dad with the other kids' fathers in the neighborhood. "My dad is bigger than yours." "My dad is stronger, faster, and smarter than your dad." The great thing is, if we are born-again believers, our Father in Heaven is the perfect Dad! He is the "Alpha and the Omega." He is the Creator of everything! He arranged the galaxies. He is so big, so powerful, so indescribable, words can't do Him justice. He is the great Healer, our Deliverer, Provider, Lover, Redeemer, and Restorer. He is exactly what you need all of the time. When we, as Christians, forget Who He is and who we are in Him, we are exactly where the enemy wants us. Our perception of God gets skewed. We say, "I just don't think it is possible that I will be healed, delivered, free from debt, or have a good job." Fill in the blank. We've all been there and that is right where the devil wants us to stay.

God wants us to know Who He is and who we are in Him! We need to ask ourselves two questions: Do we believe the Bible, or not? And do we believe Jesus is the Son of God? Hopefully, your answers are an emphatic "Yes!" So, if we believe the Word is true, we need to remind ourselves of who He is by reading His Word. Then, as we dive into the Word and it strengthens our faith--because the Word says, "faith comes by hearing and hearing by the Word of God"— we will get a better understanding of Who He is.

Once we realize His unconditional love for us and how amazing He is, then we need to understand we have His Spirit living inside us. That means there are no limits to what we can do if we are aligning ourselves up with His Word. Jesus raised people from the dead, He healed, He delivered, and He did many miracles just because He could. Greater things we will do in His Name! We need to understand who we are and who He is! Who do we represent on this Earth? Our identity is in Him. The Bible says in John 15 if we abide in Him and He abides in us we will bear much fruit. The word "abide" means to take residence or to dwell in. Have we allowed Him into every area of our lives? Have we moved in with Him? Holding nothing back? We need to understand as we allow God to "move in with us" we will start to understand how amazing He is. We will understand our own identities. Break off confusion and shut the open door in your life allowing it in, confusion is trying to steal your identity.

4. CONFUSION AND SALVATION

I want you to think of how many people you know who can't seem to receive the gospel. They can't seem to understand how much Jesus loves them. Think of that person who may have been around church their whole life but still hasn't received the gospel. There is something blocking them from receiving it. I have witnessed to many people over the last fifteen years. So many people are searching and are hungry for the truth. I mentioned earlier the Bible says we are made in His image. We have His DNA. So, there is a natural desire to get back to our true Father in Heaven. People everywhere are searching for something, but they don't know what they're searching for. They are looking for the perfect love that can only come through Jesus Christ. Unfortunately, many are seeking this fulfillment in things and people other than God like running after money, getting a better-looking wife or a more caring husband, a bigger house, a bigger promotion, or affirmation from others.

In reality, these people are seeking the love only our Father God can provide. In essence, they are trying to get back home. Have you ever noticed how many people end up going back to where they were brought up? They have a desire to get home, but the place is not physical but spiritual; it is in our intimate relationship with God. The problem is most people don't know this is what they are actually looking for.

To give you an example, I had a person working for me with whom I ate lunch for three days straight. This young man was very proud he was a father of two boys under three years old. He was also very proud of the fact he had left his wife and had a girlfriend on the side and was living by himself. Apparently, he thought he was quite the "ladies' man," or a "man's man." A real tough guy. He told me during one of our lunches he could not work Wednesday evenings because, "nothing comes between me and my boys." The Holy Spirit prompted me to confront him. I asked, "Then why are you turning your back on them and their mom if you say nothing can come between you?" By the look on his face, it was probably the first time anyone had challenged him on his immoral behavior. I told him, "You are seeking attention from someone else because you don't understand the love of Christ. You are searching for things that can only be filled by the love of Jesus. There is no relationship, no job, and no amount of money or fame that can fill that void you are looking for. You need Jesus." To make the story short, he turned his life over to Christ that day and he hasn't been the same since. Sadly, he tried reconciling with his wife, but she refused to forgive him. But his life radically changed once he understood God was the person He really needed, not another sexual partner.

What is the problem with so many people seeking the things of this world and not God? The enemy wants us to be consumed by other desires. He knows we will not be fulfilled until we experience God's love so his plan is to distract us with other things, to bring confusion, and to get us sidetracked so we can't experience the love of Christ. It is time to start dealing with this. How many people do you know who seem to be searching for something, but just don't realize it is Jesus they are searching for? You have been praying for them and it just doesn't look like they will ever understand--the prodigal son or daughter who seem to be wandering through life with no hope.

It's time to bind up the spirit of confusion as the Bible says. Jesus encourages us with the words, "whatever we bind on Earth will be bound in Heaven and whatever we loose on Earth will be loosed in Heaven." We need to bind up confusion and loose the truth so these people will experience His love. They will only stop searching when they receive Jesus in their hearts and have assurance of eternal life, the forgiveness of sins, and the redeeming love of Jesus. Let's start seeing more salvations, the prodigals coming home, addictions broken, and marriages restored. Time to move!

5. CONFUSION AND POVERTY

Do you remember the story in Jeremiah 20 about Pashhur, where he opened the door to the enemy and was sent to the land of confusion (Babylon)? God predicted in his house, family, friends including himself, would be sent there. God also mentioned he would lose everything. "God will deliver all the wealth of this city, all of its produce, all of its precious things, all of its treasure."

If we think about this story, it makes sense. Yet, if we do the same thing, we will receive the same fate as Pashhur. When we are operating out of confusion, we are going to make some poor decisions. Have you ever known a person who just can't seem to make wise decisions with their money? For example, they buy that car they can't afford, or the big house, or the most expensive clothes, or just living beyond their means. This kind of behavior can definitely be confusion, among other things. They really believe they can afford what they are doing. They take very foolish business moves. They will buy "swamp land in Florida" or spend hundreds of dollars on lottery tickets. They invest in businesses that literally have no chance of surviving. Why? They are operating out confusion. They have opened a door and the enemy has brought in confusion to bring them into bondage. The enemy loves it when we are just scraping by. We can't give to ministries. We can't give to people in need. We can't pay our bills. We begin to think God has left us. Doubt and worry monopolize our thoughts. We look at other people and start to covet what they have. Some people move to addiction to try to get away from it all.

The number one reason for divorce is money issues. He delights in dividing families. Then, very often, when children see their parents struggle financially, they become obsessed with money because they don't want this happen to them. They become workaholics. They lust after money. They are never home for their own kids. Do you see how this works? The devil is no match for our God, but he is crafty on how he attacks us. It all starts with confusion.

Deal with the open door and shut it and kick confusion out of your life! Deal with the spirit of poverty and that survival mentality. Declare it and confess it. I am no longer going to struggle financially!

6. CONFUSION AND A RELIGIOUS SPIRIT

Remember, almost every organized religion has ties to ancient Babylon (confusion). There were over 100 different gods worshipped there. The enemy wants people to chase false gods of course, but he also wants Christians to be divided. There are thousands of different Christian denominations. So many people are confused! False religion is a real problem, but why are there so many Christian denominations? We should be standing on the whole Bible. Yet, there are many different interpretations.

The spirit of religion loves to control the people and also likes to control the Holy Spirit. The enemy wants us to be bound up with the law of man. That could be why so many church services cannot deviate from what's on the program—always the same people preaching, leading worship, reading the announcements, giving the prophecies, etc. If everything is the same, we can control the Holy Spirit and people will not mess up the tidy presentation.

Unfortunately, there are many church leaders who want to control, or limit, what God wants to do during the service. At the same time, there are many church members yearning to share the giftings they've received from the Holy Spirit. But, the spirit of religion says they are not qualified, or perfect enough, or polished enough, or worthy enough to share with the congregation. This is so sad, and it is exactly what the enemy wants. People end up being spectators in the church and not fulfilling their destinies.

We squabble over different views of the Word. What are we really arguing about? We are doing exactly what the enemy wants us to do. He is great at dividing.

I feel God made it so easy for us. He gave us His Word. Remember the Bible says the Word became flesh. In other words, Jesus and the Word are the same. Let me ask you, do you only accept some of Jesus? My point is if we take all of Jesus, then why do we only accept some of the Word? Jesus is the same "yesterday, today, and forever." He did miracles yesterday, and He will do them tomorrow. There is no limit on what God can do. The only thing in life that is unchangeable is His Word! Why do we argue over His Word? It is what the enemy wants--confusion over interpretation. The bottom line is, we have Jesus as our Lord and Savior. Why are we in conflict over so many things? We need to accept the whole Word of God and walk it out.

I know a number of Christians who may view the Bible differently than I do, and sometimes we have to agree to disagree. We have Jesus in common and if someone doesn't want to accept the whole Word that is their choice. God still has a plan for them and for me. Don't let the enemy cause division in the church. Stand on the Word. If you feel you struggle with a spirit of religion, it is time to deal with it. Break confusion and shut the open door. Then deal with the religious spirit. We are only going to conquer this through Jesus!

7. CONFUSION AND PERVERSION

One of the definitions of confusion is perversion. The world is embracing what God calls perverse. The world is accepting homosexuality, same sex marriage, and transgender lifestyles. I want you to understand before you make any wrong assumptions. God loves everyone whether they are homosexual, or heterosexual, and we need to do the same without endorsing the lifestyle. I just want to explain why I think this is so prevalent now.

Among millennials the amount of people who identify themselves with the LGBT community has doubled. Over eight percent of millennials and 4.5% (5.1% of women and 3.9% men) percent of every person in the U.S. identify this way. This is growing at such a fast rate. Men want to be women, women want to be men, and some people want to be both. God calls this perversion according to His Word and it is time to turn the tide on this spirit of confusion.

A CALL TO CLARITY

This is still a controversial topic; despite the fact it is becoming more and more acceptable. We must stand on the Word of God! That is not the way God designed us. God will not go against His own Word. They were not "born that way." God stands on His Word. We all know someone who may be struggling with their sexual identity. We need to bind the spirit of confusion in their life and show them the love of Christ. God needs us to embrace His Word and His love!

8. CONFUSION AND REBELLION

Rebellion is the same as witchcraft according to the Word.

I Samuel 15:23 (NKJV)

"For rebellion is as the sin of witchcraft, and stubbornness is as iniquity and idolatry. Because you have rejected the Word of the Lord, He also has rejected you from being king."

Rebellion and witchcraft are tied together. Babylon, the city of confusion, rebelled against God and embraced the god named Marduk. He was the main god of Babylon and was the god of magic, or the god of chaos (confusion).

Rebellion is the foundation of sin. It is the exact opposite of what God wants from us. 1 Samuel 15:22 says: *"Behold, to obey is better than sacrifice."* He calls us to obey His Word! The devil convinces us to stop obeying God's word. The devil longs for us to be disobedient towards God.

RESULTS OF CONFUSION IN OUR LIVES

Rebellion means an act of violent or open resistance to an established government or ruler. When we are walking in rebellion, we are resisting our God, resisting the Kingdom of God and His government. There are consequences to disobedience. Not because God wants to bring some type of harsh discipline on us but because He wants to protect us from the enemy. He knows disobedience opens the door to the enemy. Think of how many things your parents told you to keep you safe: *Look both ways before crossing the street, Don't climb so high in that tree, Don't put your hand on the hot stove. Don't run in a parking lot.* When my oldest sister was younger, she wouldn't stay out of the road and my mom tied her on a leash to the front tree. Now please don't turn my mom into child protective services: she is going to be ninety and things were a lot different back then. My parents were great parents and there were seven of us. She probably was a little tired of chasing all my siblings around. She was just trying to protect my sister. I call that tree the "tree of life." Obedience protects us from the enemy running us over. God, of course, wants us to be tied to Him voluntarily, not forcibly.

I had a dog named Buddy when I was younger. Buddy was so fast he could catch squirrels. Afterwards, he would terminate them if you know what I mean. Buddy's strategy was interesting. He would sit by that same tree in the front yard and act totally uninterested in the squirrels. Then, when the squirrels strayed far enough from that tree (or refuge) he would bolt after them and catch them. This is exactly what the enemy does when we stray too far from

God, who is our Tree of Life and refuge. He roams around and waits for his big chance to bring chaos.

Time to shut the door to confusion. Shut the open door and keep the enemy out. Deal with rebellion and fulfill your destiny.

9. CONFUSION AND IDOL WORSHIP

Babylon was where idol worship was deeply entrenched. They had over 100 different gods. Confusion causes idol worship. This is when we lose focus on how awesome God is and start chasing after other things to take His place. When we place worship on something, or someone other than God, it is an idol. This nation struggles with so many idols. We place money, fame, careers, relationships, sports, and even celebrities in place of our relationship with God. We can look at sports as the end all. We worship movie stars and music entertainers, and we spend thousands of dollars following them around the country. We take days off work to see them.

We would rather let our children play by themselves, so we don't miss the game, or show. We may invest thousands of dollars trying to turn our kids into the next superstar. I have done some coaching in the past and it is amazing how whacked out some of the parents get. Some of these kids are really uncoordinated and really hate sports but their parents are determined their kid be the next shortstop for the New York Yankees. Rather than allowing their child to walk in the gifts God has given them, they are forced to play sports. Others, who are actually good, get burned out because of the high expectations of their parents--the camps, the travel teams, the weekend practices. Very often this child's siblings suffer because the one child is the "chosen one."

Money is another thing people may put very high on their list. We chase the almighty dollar. We look at money as the answer to all our problems. Have you ever asked yourself: *If I could just have a little more money, everything would be okay?* How many times have we asked: *If I could only get a little more Jesus and His presence, everything would be okay?* Do you see what I am saying? I think we've all been there. I hate to tell you this, but this is "the love of money" and it is idol worship.

Career can be another idol. We place our careers in place of God, family, and friends. We tell our kids we just can't make it home to play with them night after night. We're making excuses and missing out on the best years of their lives. We may give God a couple hours a week but is not enough and we overlook what is really important. We must advance our career because that will make us "complete." This is an idol.

Believe it or not, we can even make ministry an idol in our lives. Yet, if ministry comes before our personal relationship with God, it is an idol. Our first ministry is to our family. When we consistently put our ministry before our family, can be a sign it is an idol.

Kick confusion out and deal with your idols. Slam the open doors shut!

10. CONFUSION AND DISCERNMENT

We all need godly discernment for every aspect of our lives. Look at all the big decisions we've made in our lives and even the little ones we make daily. We need His wisdom and guidance for relationships, jobs, ministry, travel, and so many things.

When I was young, I really needed some guidance. I remember trying to decide where I should go to college after high school and what I should major in. I really had no idea what I wanted to do. Think of how much easier it would have been if I was thinking clearly. I wasn't saved yet and walking with the Lord, so the enemy could definitely bring in confusion. My dad didn't want to influence me or my siblings at all, so he allowed all seven of us to make our own decisions. I remember saying out loud to anyone who would listen, "I have no idea what I want to do!" Many people have that same feeling. Finally, I decided to become a diesel mechanic and ended up being successful, but I always wondered if I went to college, rather than a technical school, how that would have affected my life. Maybe if I had gone to a school where I could have played sports, which I loved, I would have chosen a different career.

Have you ever looked back and wondered, *what if?* Now I will say this, God knows the beginning from the

end, and He wasn't shocked by my decision. And I
what I did for thirty years.

Just think how important having discernment is; i.
the ability to judge a situation from God's perspective. Are
you judging situations well? How are you handling that big
decision? Think about relationships. Should I date that person? Whom should I marry? Should I become close friends
with that person? The negative warning signs are very often
there, but we don't see them, or sense them. I know we all
know someone who dated a person who just wasn't right
for them. Maybe that person was verbally abusive to them,
or unfaithful. Maybe they were lazy, crude, rude, or even
have a substance abuse problem. Why then can their friends
and family see it, but they can't? It is poor discernment,
poor judgment. Sadly, often those same people go so far as
to marry that person! Sometimes we receive advice more
easily about our cars than we do about relationships, which
can be life-altering!

What about your career decisions? How will you make
a living? Where should you work? Do you start your own
business? If you do, should you go into business with a
partner, or by yourself? Should you hire this contractor or
find someone else? I was working for a construction equipment dealer and I was doing well but I wondered, *what do I
do now after fourteen years?* I had advanced in my depart-
ment as far as I could go. *What's next?*

Meanwhile, my wife was encouraging me to start my
own heavy equipment repair business. She was walking in

godly discernment and she felt strongly I needed to start something up. She had a very good job, but she felt like God wanted her to stay home with our children. She was nine months pregnant with our second child when she gave her notice at her job. Given the circumstances, starting my own business did not make a lot of sense in the natural because it could take years before I started making a good profit. But God had other plans. I was asked to do something unethical by my new boss and I came home that night and told Kim I was quitting. This meant both of us were without jobs and we had two little ones at home and all the bills to go with it.

I immediately started up the business and I can honestly say we never missed a payment. She had heard from the Lord! She was right (my wife will love me for admitting this). For the record, I would have never started my own business without her discernment. She really sensed I needed to press forward. Thank you, Lord, for discernment at just the right moment! Some jobs we are considering may involve moving out of the area, or non-stop travel. Neither of these options are necessarily bad, but we need discernment before we accept the position for the sake of our family.

We can apply this principle to every area of our lives. Here is one, how about answering the call of God for ministry? My wife, Kim, and I were involved in Christian service for many years before we sought to be ordained as ministers in 2016. Surprisingly, our kids said, "It's about time!" They saw it coming, but it took us years to answer the call. The spirit of confusion wants to breakdown the communication between us and the Father.

Spiritual discernment is essential to have as Christians for whatever situation we find ourselves in and for all the decisions we need to make. We need His guidance to position us where He needs us. Deal with confusion, shut the door, and kick confusion out.

11. CONFUSION AND DOUBT

This is how the enemy works: he creates confusion. We start doubting Who God is and who we are in Him, and that doubt undermines our faith. The Word is very clear on how important faith is to God.

Hebrews 11:6 (NKJV)

"But without faith it is impossible to please Him, for he who comes to God must believe that He is, and that He is a rewarder of those who diligently seek Him." Think about that for a minute. The Word says it is impossible to please Him without faith! Impossible! Unable! We can't! Not happening! God has great pleasure when we have faith--when we have unshakeable faith. In other words, we please the Father when we see victory through Him in every circumstance!

What pleases the enemy? When we don't trust God and exercise our faith. The enemy loves it when we go through life looking at defeat in every situation. The enemy takes delight when we doubt and are full of unbelief, and we walk around depressed and broken. It is all tied together. Lack of faith brings so many negative things into our lives. On the contrary, we put a big smile on God's face when we walk in faith and keep our heads held high.

When we walk in faith and diligently seeking Him, we are not only pleasing Him, but we also are setting ourselves up to receive His rewards for doing so. The word "rewarder" in this verse means "one who pays wages." God wants to bless us for our faith in Him. The Lord brings a blessing, and the devil brings a curse! Are you lacking in faith? Do you struggle with doubt? I want faith that moves the mountains in my life and yours. We never want to limit God in our lives. When we lack faith, we limit God—*we* are responsible for limiting what He can do! Just think, the only thing in this world that can derail our destiny is…us. God is more than willing. He just wants us to believe and trust in Him!

It is time to deal with doubt, worry, strife, and lack of faith. You know the drill: deal with the open doors, then renounce and repent of all the doubt, worry, and lack of faith in Jesus's Name, and confusion will go. Romans 12:3 says God has dealt to each one of us "a measure of faith." He says faith is in you whether you think you have it, or not. Don't allow the enemy to steal your faith. Don't allow him to place limits in your life. Faith is in you! Time to move our mountains and walk in our destinies!

12. CONFUSION AND CHAOS

Do you sometimes feel that your life is too busy and overwhelming? Not enough hours in a day? We've all been there. Work is constantly asking for more of our time. If you have children, they always have some kind of event to attend--soccer, band, birthday parties, you name it. This is not to say these things are bad, but it is easy to over commit ourselves sometimes because we don't want to say no, which leads to added stress we don't need. The enemy wants to bring disorder and chaos in our lives. In this busyness of life, we become stressed, angry, edgy, and we usually don't sleep well. We need His peace. The meaning of the word chaos is *"complete disorder and confusion."* Does that sound familiar?

How can we possibly be doing what God wants in our lives if we are in "complete disorder?" We can't be the spouses or parents we've been called to be if our lives are in chaos. Most importantly, chaos will eat up our quality time with the Lord, which obviously is the plan of the enemy.

Think about your time with God. Does it suffer because of this chaos in your life? Think about your family time as a husband, wife, or parent. Are you spending the quality time needed? Are you choosing work over quality time with God, your spouse, and your children? Can you make room for the important things?

This is exactly what the enemy wants for your life—to be pushed around by too many commitments instead of abiding in God's peace on His schedule. About ten years ago, the Lord pressed on my heart that there is a major battle for all of us over time. In fact, we are often so busy we don't even see it happening. The enemy is so sly and comes in the back door and, before we even know what is going on, we are overwhelmed; our kids feel neglected, and our spouse has checked out of the marriage. All of a sudden, our family's destiny has been altered.

God has said in His Word that He will give peace in our lives.

I Corinthians 14:33 (NKJV):

"For God is not the author of confusion but of peace, as in all the churches of the saints." I repeat. God is not the author of confusion, chaos, and disorder. He is the Author of peace! He has peace for you and me and He wants us to walk in it. But we need to seek Him for His peace. Do you want to take a deep breath and rest? I know so many people who need a break from the chaos in their lives. Why do we allow the enemy to dictate our schedule? I know we all have responsibilities, but when we forget to put God first, we allow the enemy to bring in his plans. Suddenly, we are under duress. As the Word says in Matthew 6:33 (NKJV):

"But seek first the kingdom of God and His righteous-

ness, and all these things shall be added to you." He calls us to seek Him first, not second, third, or fourth. Have we made Him the number one priority in our lives?

He will bring in peace as the Word says in Philippians 4:7 (NKJV): "*and the peace of God, which surpasses all understanding, will guard your hearts and minds through Christ Jesus.*" He will give us peace that surpasses all understanding. We will have so much peace in our lives we won't even be able to comprehend it. How does that sound? There is nothing like waking up in the morning and looking forward to the day and going to bed without any chaos. How about this change? Instead of moaning, "Oh God" every morning and facing the day with dread, how about confessing, "Thank you, Lord, for the great day You have planned for me!" You know what you need to do: Shut the door and kick confusion out and invite in God's peace!

13. CONFUSION AND REJECTION/UNWORTHINESS

This goes back to identity. The enemy wants us to believe that we have been rejected by God. If we listen to those lies and are conflicted in our minds of who we are in Christ, it will gain a foothold in us. Confusion is constantly messing with us. That is why it is so important to allow God's Word to penetrate our hearts, not just our minds. It says in the Word "*out of the abundance of your heart the mouth speaks.*" This can be good and bad. If we allow the enemy to penetrate our hearts, we will be bitter and have all kinds of rejection issues. Proverbs 4:23 says (NKJV): *"Keep your heart with all diligence, for out of it spring the issues of life."* We need to come into agreement with God and what He says about us.

You are worthy! You haven't been rejected! Deal with this and move into your destiny!

SOMETHING TO THINK ABOUT.

How does confusion affect our everyday lives?

If you are struggling in any of these areas, it could be confusion and now is the time to deal with it.

CHAPTER 6

Confusion and the Seven Mountains of Influence

The Bible talks about the Seven Mountains in Revelation 17.

1 Then one of the seven angels who had the seven bowls came and talked with me, saying to me, "Come, I will show you the judgment of the great harlot who sits on many waters, 2 with whom the kings of the earth committed fornication, and the inhabitants of the earth were made drunk with the wine of her fornication."

3 So he carried me away in the Spirit into the wilderness. And I saw a woman sitting on a scarlet beast which was full of names of blasphemy, having seven heads and ten horns. 4 The woman was arrayed in purple and scarlet, and adorned with gold and precious stones and pearls, having in her hand a golden cup full of abominations and the filthiness of her fornication. 5And on her forehead a name was written:

MYSTERY, BABYLON THE GREAT,

THE MOTHER OF HARLOTS

AND OF THE ABOMINATIONS

OF THE EARTH.

6 I saw the woman, drunk with the blood of the saints and with the blood of the martyrs of Jesus. And when I saw her, I marveled with great amazement...

9"Here is the mind which has wisdom: *The seven heads are seven mountains on which the woman sits."*

Revelation 17:14 (NKJV)

"These will make war with the Lamb, and the Lamb will overcome them, for He is Lord of lords and King of kings; and those who are with Him are called, chosen, and faithful."

Let's review what it says in these verses. In 17:2 it says the kings (leaders) have committed fornication with her (Babylon/confusion). We (all inhabitants) were made drunk with her (confusion) fornication. It will affect everyone. Verse three says this woman (confusion) has names of blasphemy on her. She (confusion) blasphemes the Lord! Verse four talks about how she (confusion) is adorned with jewels. She looks good to us. The enemy will convince us what he/she is doing is good. This is exactly how the media works. It convinces us good is evil and evil is good. Verse five says on her forehead Babylon (confusion) the great is the mother of harlots and the abominations of the earth.

Confusion is the mother of abomination, or hatred of the things of God. Verse six talks about how the woman (confusion) is drunk with the blood of the saints. It (confusion) destroys the saints. It takes them out. Verse nine says this woman is sitting on the seven mountains, which, I believe, are the Seven Mountains of influence. This is where the enemy wants to sit, on every mountain influencing the whole of society at every level. The verse says she (confusion) will make war with the Lamb (God) but it also says God will overcome! This tells us there is a battle, but we win because we are standing with Jesus! Read the end of the Bible and you will see we are victorious! There is nothing to fear because He is in us is greater than he that is against us!

Now let's look at what the enemy is trying to influence.

The Seven Mountains of influence are the following:

- Business

- Government

- Media

- Arts and Entertainment

- Education

- Religion

- Family

The Body of Christ should be influencing these mountains. After all, we serve the God created everything. The word for the Christian Church in the Greek is "Ekkelsia." The meaning of this word is "governing body." God wants us to influence the world with His Word and His love. Just imagine what the world would be like if that was the case. The enemy, however, definitely doesn't want this to happen. I will give a quick summary of each mountain, but I suggest you study up on them on your own. There are some very good teachings on this subject. I will explain how confusion gets tied to these mountains after I give the summary.

BUSINESS MOUNTAIN

The Business Mountain is the source of income for most people. It is where goods and services are exchanged. It is crucial that the Business Mountain runs ethically and honestly. The problem is many businesses do things illegally--tax evasion, money laundering, etc. There are trillions and trillions of dollars that run through these businesses.

CONFUSION AND THE SEVEN MOUNTAINS OF INFLUENCE

Did you know there is an estimated two trillion dollars paid "under the table" **every year?** That means two trillion dollars go untaxed annually. At a 15% tax rate, which is low to many Americans, this comes to 300 billion dollars owed to the government. That is just a small portion of what goes on. I had my own business for years and I was regularly asked to do illegal transactions by my customers. Of course, I didn't do those things but if I witnessed it in my business, I'm sure it goes on elsewhere. We need sold out Christians to be operating businesses in this country. We need to get serious in our country about companies running properly. If this happened, I am convinced, we would see ministries thrive, the gospel reaching around the world, and poverty becoming a thing of the past. Awesome!

GOVERNMENT MOUNTAIN

Wow! This is a doozy! The basic functions of the U.S. government, listed in the constitution, are to "form a more perfect union, to establish justice, to ensure domestic tranquility, to provide for the common defense, to promote the general welfare and to secure the blessings of liberty."

Now, I want you to think of the many illegal things the government does regularly. I'm not trying to stir you up, but the news is constantly highlighting some politician who got paid off, or was in the news for lying, stealing, or cheating. This is a major problem, and if you were to ask the average person if they trusted the government, I believe, most would say "NO." Does this sound like what the constitution describes our government should look like? It is so sad. Many politicians have no idea of what it's like to work a normal job. When this country was first founded, however, it was normal for townspeople to enlist an honest local farmer to run for office, which he would do in addition to managing his farm. Today, we have professional politicians who don't value what the constitution says, or truly understand those who work regular jobs. They are about their own agenda. Yet, our nation was founded on Christian principles and the reason, I believe, we grew into such a powerful and blessed nation in such a short time is because we honored God.

Look at when we removed prayer from the schools. That is when teenage pregnancies went through the roof, SAT scores dropped, divorce rates went way up, abortion became the law of the land, and homosexuality became an alternate lifestyle. Unfortunately, this nation is doing its best to drive God away. We need sold out Christians to run for office and to become leaders in government to turn this nation around.

MEDIA MOUNTAIN

The most common platforms for mass media are newspapers, magazines, radio, television, and the internet. They influence us in so many ways. Their job is to pass on information to us so we can make wise decisions, wise purchases, and educate us about medical issues. Another other thing they do is give us the world news and what is happening on our planet.

News agencies are supposed to present the news without being bias towards their own agenda. Yet today, these agencies are a real problem because they present the news only from their unique perspective. Some news networks tell viewers and listeners up front they are biased while others pretend they are presenting the truth, "the whole truth and nothing but the truth" but please help us God. Many report negative things on the political party they don't like and will ignore anything negative about their own party. But where is the network that gives both sides of the issues? This is vital in today's world. Some social commentators say we are so polarized today because everyone listens to their own version of the truth. So many people are easily slanted by the media. They are being unethical when they take sides in their reporting regardless of the facts. We need honest journalism, so the people are informed properly.

The Bible says that Satan is the "prince of the power of the air." Ephesians 2:2 (NKJV) says:

"...in which you once walked according to the course of this world, according to the prince of the power of the air, the spirit who now works in the sons of disobedience."

Think about this verse. He oversees the power of the air. There is great power in the airways. Remember, however, even though the enemy is "prince of the air," Jesus is "King of kings and "Lord of Lords." Jesus says we have "all authority over the enemy." Our challenge is to run the media.

The word "media" comes from the word "medium." Now the word medium means – "someone, or something, in the middle." The air is the medium that conveys sound, or a channel or system of communication.

This is what we need to understand. The truth must be delivered through communication. The enemy wants to deliver lies and cause division. If we allow the enemy to run our lines of communication, we will be continually pounded by lies. It isn't just the nightly news; it's what we read in the newspapers, magazines, and on the internet, all of which includes a lot of deception and lies.

Think of how the person in the middle can distort the truth. Do you remember playing the telephone game in kindergarten? You would tell the first child in the front one thing and he, or she, would tell the next child and so on down the line until the last child received the message. Eventually, the message would be totally distorted by the time it reached the last child because each child would only communicate what they thought they heard. That is what it is like when we allow the enemy to be in the middle of our media. He is the father of lies and loves to tell them--twisting the truth and pushing people away from God and His Word is his MO (modus operandi). Again, the enemy wants us to see good as evil and evil as good!

We, as believers, need to pray for this Media Mountain

so sold-out Christians will be leaders on this mountain. When we hear news that doesn't line up with the Word of God and tries to slant public opinion against God and His plan, we need to stand up. We need to keep the enemy from manipulating us. He wants us to turn from God! So many Christians can be easily turned to the enemy's agenda through this method. Just take abortion, for instance. The enemy has convinced this nation it is awful if you take a stand against it. There you are taking away a woman's right to choose. Ponder this for a second. The Bible says in Isaiah 5:20 (NKJV): *"Woe to those who call evil good, and good evil; Who put darkness for light, and light for darkness; Who put bitter for sweet, and sweet for bitter!"*

I'm not sure how anyone can say killing a baby is good. I'm sure if I had a puppy mill and I was doing the same thing to puppies they would have me in jail. I'm not saying it's right to abuse animals, but I feel that animals today have better rights than babies in the womb. The devil has twisted the truth and convinced many in this country that abortion is a woman's right. So sad! We need to not be afraid to call evil what it is. We need to position sold-out Christians on this mountain. We need to deal with confusion on this mountain and ask for clarity and truth. We need to influence with the love of Christ and His Words.

ARTS AND ENTERTAINMENT MOUNTAIN

This mountain is so influential. This has so much influence on our children. They want to be like the famous pop singer, famous athlete, or movie star. The movie business is pushing R-rated movies at a much higher rate, even though statistics show they usually make two to three times more money on PG- and G-rated movies. How does that make sense? There is something very wrong with that. They would rather sacrifice profits by pushing God-dishonoring entertainment than succeeding financially. Most of them are full of sex and graphic violence. Try to tell me that the enemy isn't behind this agenda. The movie industry will blackball actors or actresses who are outspoken Christians. Unfortunately, they have a tremendous amount of money to push their agenda. The moral decay in this arena is so pronounced to me. When I was a kid, there were so many wholesome movies and TV shows. The comedy shows also were so funny, but very clean. My wife and I were saying just the other day; everyone back then seemed so talented. They could dance, sing, act and were so funny. (Remember Bing Crosby, Bob Hope, and Jack Benny?). Where are they today? The enemy is very hard at work.

Look at the billion-dollar gaming industry and how many of these video games are polluting our kids' minds. We see kids are reenacting murder, sex, and all types of violence, thus creating a numbness to these things. It is heartbreaking. When I was a kid, we used to play all types of sports outside every day, or had adventures in the woods, or we played games like capture the flag. We went fishing, played street hockey, tag, football, and baseball. The last thing on our mind was to sit on a chair and stare at a screen for hours and hours. This is the enemy doing his work again.

The sports industry is another huge business. It can influence so many people. The athletes are worshipped as idols. Yet, they can also be quickly shunned for speaking about their Christian views. I distinctly remember the league making a special rule so the athletes couldn't write Bible verses on their bodies. On the other hand, many of them can act crudely or say awful things with apparently no repercussions. This is more of the same. We need to get God back in this country in every area.

EDUCATION MOUNTAIN

Education is supposed to teach us skills and knowledge. A country's knowledge can be passed on from generation to generation through education. Education can mold a nation and society for good or bad. This is why it is so important to have sold-out Christians on this mountain.

The problem is, as a nation, we have allowed our public-school teachers to educate our children with the principles of this world, instead of with the Word of God. The Bible was used as a textbook in schools up until the early 1900s. It was used for teaching morals and good character. It was also used for history and spelling. In fact, prayer was used in every classroom until it was removed by the Supreme Court in 1963. That is when things started going downhill. Listen to the results of doing so: Criminal arrests of teens are up 150 percent. Teen suicides are up 450 percent. Illegal drug use up 6,000 percent! Child abuse up

2,300 percent! Divorce rates up 350 percent! SAT scores have also plummeted even though they have made the test easier. Violent crime is up 350 percent. Teenage pregnancy is up 500 percent. In 1947, only 12 percent of teenagers felt premarital sex was okay. In 2017, 85 percent of teens felt it was acceptable. Single parent homes up 500 percent! The U.S. spends more money than any other country on education, but we are rated 17th in the world. Something is up! When looking at college students, statistics show 70 percent of Christians going on to higher education will walk away from their faith before they graduate. In other words, if the high school education does not take out Christian students, college indoctrination will take it a notch higher!

If looking at those results of removing prayer from school doesn't open our eyes, I'm not sure what will. The Bible says this:

Proverbs 2:5 (NKJV)

"Then you will understand the fear of the Lord and find the knowledge of God." We need to find reverence for the Lord if we want to discover His knowledge.

Proverbs 2:6 (NKJV)

"For the Lord gives wisdom; From His mouth come knowledge and understanding…"

Proverbs 2:7 (NKJV)

"He stores up sound wisdom for the upright; He is a shield to those who walk uprightly…"

God's wisdom is what we all need. He will give us knowledge and understanding. He promises us He will shield us.

Yet, we decided as a nation we didn't need God or His Word to help us educate our children. We told God, "You are not welcomed in our schools: We can educate our children better than You." This is a major issue. Consider how the young people are thinking right now. Many of them have deviated from God's morality, have poor work ethics, and feel they are entitled to free higher education and other benefits from the government. God's heart and mine, however, is to see them fulfill their God-given destinies without making government a capital G.

Think of the damage removing prayer has done? It's time to get prayer back in the schools and the Bible back into its rightful place.

Proverbs 22:6 (NKJV)

"Train up a child in the way he should go, and when he is old he will not depart from it." To train or teach your children up is to get them going in the right direction. Do you think the way of the world is the direction you want your children to go? Or, is it God's way? God's way has proven to be the best way by far. Jesus says, "Bring the children to Me." He has the knowledge. He has the guidance. He will give them security. He will respond to all of their questions. He says, "I have not rejected you."

Children are struggling. They may feel insecure and unloved because we decided to remove God from their classrooms. We need to give them security again. Let us deal with the confusion that seems to be on this mountain. Invite God's people to lead the education system and watch the education system prosper again. We will see things change for the better. Victory will be ours!

RELIGION MOUNTAIN

Every part of the world believes in some type of superior being. We know as Christians, however, there is only one true God. What causes so many different beliefs? It is obviously confusion. Let's look at the Christian church alone. There are thousands of different Christian denominations. God made it simple. Read His Word and live out His Word. We need the church to pull together and come into agreement with His Word and each other. The enemy thrives on the division he has caused by all these different denominations. Just think of what the church could accomplish by moving together. You would see the fulfillment of the great commission!

Mark 16:15 (NKJV)

"And He said to them, "Go into all the world and preach the gospel to every creature."

Mark 16:17 (NKJV)

"And these signs will follow those who believe: In My

name they will cast out demons; they will speak with new tongues…"

Mark 16:18 (NKJV)

"They will take up serpents; and if they drink anything deadly, it will by no means hurt them; they will lay hands on the sick, and they will recover."

Let me ask you this; Are we preaching the gospel all over the world and to everyone? There is a huge mission field in the United States alone. Just think of the billions of people in India and China entrenched in false religions. They need the gospel so badly. What type of signs are following you? Are you seeing signs and miracles following you as the Bible says it should?

When was the last time you cast out a demon in Jesus's Name? When was the last time you spoke in a new tongue? How about this one, when was the last time you laid hands on the sick and saw them recover. He said these are the type of things that should follow us. In other words, we shouldn't be following the miracles; they should be following us. That is one of the biggest problems with the church. We chase after miracles instead of His Presence. We want the miracle. We need the miracle, but He said they should follow us! This is what the Church should look like! Get this confusion off this mountain and call in the clarity of God.

FAMILY MOUNTAIN

The family is the single most important influence on us as individuals, and for our nation as a whole. If a child grows up without a good, loving family foundation, he/she will, no doubt, face greater obstacles. Family affects all facets of life. Just think how the enemy wants the family divided. Dysfunctional households can damage its members. Without Christ, these people are more likely to be in jail, more likely to have an addiction issue, more likely to need public assistance, and more likely to have relationship issues. These consequences affect us all as a society.

My wife and I have sometimes ministered to homeless people. One of the questions we like to ask them is: "What is your story? Why are you living on the street? What happened?" Usually, although they may not see it initially, the root cause is rejection. Most of the time, it starts with a tough home life and takes a downward spiral from there. The mom or dad left; or one or both of their parents were abusive physically or verbally to them. The abuse then plants seeds of rejection that go deeply into them. They feel unworthy, overlooked, and abandoned! These people very often suffer with mental disorders such as depression. The enemy loves to attack the mind. Remember we are all made in His image: We are all precious in His sight. This is why Christian mentors are so vital.

I remember coaching my son's soccer team when he was very young. Some of the kids were a real handful, but as the season progressed, they really enjoyed being there. I am a motivator and God has given me a gift to see things in children and adults that they may not see in themselves. So, I could see things in these young kids. I could tell many of them didn't hear encouragement at home. In fact, many of the parents of my team members would just drop their kids off and run rather than taking the time to watch them practice or play in an official game. I understand the importance of work, but it struck me how few parents actually invested their time in their children.

As the season progressed and I concentrated on encouraging each player, I was amazed how much their behavior and their playing skills improved. I remember saying goodbye to the kids at their last game and I recall one little girl, who was by far the most improved in terms of her behavior, come running up to me and give me a big hug. She pleaded with me, "Will you be my coach next year?" It wasn't that I did anything special, I just spoke positive things over all the kids. I believe they could see the light of the Lord in me, and they enjoyed being lifted up. We need to volunteer and shine the light to people around us. The world needs this, and some families need more support than others.

When I owned my business, I could tell when my employees were struggling at home. If they had problems with their children or their spouse, it would cause trouble at work. The enemy wants to bring confusion and division into every area of your lives. Family division will destroy ministries, businesses, relationships, and more. When the family is doing well, it affects everything and overflows into the towns, cities, states, and nation.

A CALL TO CLARITY

Deuteronomy 6:6 (NKJV) says,

"And these words which I command you today shall be in your heart."

Deuteronomy 6:7 (NKJV)

"You shall teach them diligently to your children and shall talk of them when you sit in your house, when you walk by the way, when you lie down, and when you rise up."

God wants His Word to be part of our everyday lives. Your children need to be taught His Word, or guess what? The enemy will fill that void if we don't and what the enemy teaches always bears bad fruit. Let's kick confusion out of our households and invite His clarity through His Word.

SOMETHING TO THINK ABOUT.

What are the Seven Mountains of influence?

Can you see how confusion has affected these?

We need to pray for clarity over these mountains on a regular basis.

Think about getting involved to make difference in these mountains. Bring His Kingdom to your workplace.

CHAPTER 7

Jesus is the Answer! Time For Clarity!

So far, we have talked about confusion being a tool the enemy uses to bring all kinds of mayhem into our lives-- bringing destruction and all types of problems. We have talked about open doors in which we need to take very seriously so we can shut them. We've talked about how the enemy wants to get in charge of the Seven Mountains of influence to affect every one of us. One thing we haven't gone over is how Jesus and His Word have all the answers we need and will crush this confusion in our lives!

One thing I am going to make very clear is God is not the author of confusion but of peace. He is the God of clarity!

I Corinthians 14:33 (NKJV)

"For God is not the author of confusion but of peace, as

in all the churches of the saints."

He says He brings us peace. If you are struggling with confusion, I have great news for you. God will give you peace! Confusion is not from God! And there is something else you should know. You have the "mind of Christ," if you have received Jesus Christ in your heart.

I Corinthians 2:16 (NKJV)

"For who has known the mind of the Lord that he may instruct Him? But we have the mind of Christ."

We have the mind of Christ! Let me ask you something, do you think Jesus ever gets confused? Do you think He is up in Heaven looking down with his hands on His head saying to himself, "Oh no! What am I going to do?" He is always in control, always clear-minded, and always has a plan. So, if we have the mind of Christ, why then do we operate out of our carnal minds? We all struggle with it, but we have stop operating out of the carnal mind. We have to be Kingdom-minded and not carnally minded. We cannot accomplish what God has called us to do if we are thinking carnally. The carnal mind is selfish! To give you an example, let's look at my medical condition. If I analyze it with a carnal mind and what the doctors tell me, I have no hope, but with God's perspective, or the mind of Christ, I see myself totally healed and set free.

I Peter 4:1 (NKJV)

"Therefore, since Christ suffered for us in the flesh, arm

yourselves also with the same mind,

We need to arm ourselves with His mind."

That takes effort. You don't arm a gun without loading the ammunition. The same goes for arming yourself with the mind of Christ. What is our spiritual ammunition? It is the Word of God! We need to load our mind up with His truth. He has all the answers to every question. Soak in His Word and it will transform us and change our perspective on every situation. It changes our carnal minds to a Kingdom mind. We should not complain about our circumstances if we are not allowing the Word to transform us. Reading and spending time in God's Word is essential to arming ourselves with the mind of Christ. What kind of ammunition are you arming yourself with? The enemy wants you to arm yourself with his lies, so you are weak and feel like you have no purpose. He wants us to be confused or conflicted in our minds.

Romans 15:5 (NKJV)

"Now may the God of patience and comfort grant you to be like-minded toward one another, according to Christ Jesus, 6 that you may with one mind and one mouth glorify the God and Father of our Lord Jesus Christ."

When we operate out of the Kingdom mindset, we will be like-minded towards each other. Doesn't that sound great! The church being of one mind, one plan, and one goal to glorify His name and fulfill His calling! It says in verse six "one mind and one mouth" to glorify our God--

not exalting in our own agenda, or our ministry, or ourselves. Let us be one under Him!

Remember how this confusion thing started at the Tower of Babel--confusion came in because of the sin of pride and the people seeking to exalt themselves, not God. The Lord wants us to speak one language and that is the language of His love, which is the greatest gift. The enemy wants us to speak the language of pride, arrogance, deceit, idol worship, envy, and rebellion. The key is operating out of the mind of Christ.

If you are having trouble with this, please speak His Word over yourself. Tell the enemy-the same Spirit raised Jesus from the grave lives inside you! Tell the enemy you are, from now on, going to operate out of the mind of Christ and no longer out of the carnal mind. Can you picture Jesus lying? Going back on His Word? I don't think so! Seeking His will, not ours!

Hebrews 10:35,36 (NKJV)

"Therefore do not cast away your confidence, which has great reward. 36 For you have need of endurance, so that after you have done the will of God, you may receive the promise."

This is one of my favorite verses. When we are confused, we lack confidence, and we lose our identity. We need endurance so we can accomplish the good works He has ordained for us to walk in. The biggest flashing neon sign in this verse from Hebrews is at the end. It says,

AFTER we have done the will of God, we will receive the promise. AFTER! I am not saying you can work your way to Heaven because we can only get there through Jesus. What I am saying is there are many promises in the Bible we will not see unless we change our mindset. It isn't about what God is going to do for us, it should be about what we can do for Him today! Jesus was always about His Father's business.

I was in prayer one morning and the Lord spoke to my heart and said, "Boy, you have quite the list! When was the last time you said, 'Lord, what would you like me to do for You today?'" God wasn't saying I don't want to bless you or answer your prayers, what He was saying was make Me your priority every day and you will see the blessings the prayers answered, and My will accomplished on this Earth!

This is key to seeing breakthrough in your life. Chase after His will and His Presence. He pressed on my heart that so many people chase the miracles and blessings more than His will and presence. He asked Me a real tough question once, He said, "If you had to choose one thing, your healing, or My Presence, what would your answer be?" Let me make this very clear, He was not saying I had to choose. He wanted me to think and evaluate where my heart was really at. Was I really with Him? Or was I just someone who was in it for myself? I know so many people who get so mad at God because they say, "He doesn't answer my prayers." What I would say to people like this: "When was the last time you said, 'Lord, what can I do for you?'" We can chase the blessings and miracles more than His Presence.

Let's get our priorities straight and daily invite His Presence into our lives and seek His will, not ours, and then we will see the miracles and blessings.

SOMETHING TO THINK ABOUT.

How is Jesus the answer?

How does His Word set us free?

Write down the verses that have the most influence on you and read them. Allow them to penetrate deep into your heart.

CHAPTER 8

Let's Get Cleaned Up!

First, we need to break off any bondage of sin in our lives. Here are the open doors we talked about earlier: Pride, Idol Worship, Rebellion, Religious Spirit, Unrepentance, Disobedience, Envy, Jealousy, Self-Seeking, Perversion, Shame, and Lying- (or going back on your word). We need to be free from all bondage. Let's go back to the Word of God! We are free in Jesus. There should not be anything in this world that holds us back.

- John 8:36 *"Therefore if the Son makes you free, you shall be free indeed."*

- *Luke 4:18 "The Spirit of the Lord is upon Me, Because He has anointed Me To preach the gospel to the poor; He has sent Me to heal the brokenhearted, to proclaim liberty to the captives And recovery of sight to the blind, To set at liberty those who are oppressed..."*

Let me ask you, "Has the Son set you free?" I will

answer this for you. Yes, He has! If you have accepted Jesus Christ as your Lord and Savior, then you are free! He proclaims or declares liberty over you! He is going to give you a vision for your future. The verse isn't just saying He will heal blind people (which He will), He is giving you a hope and a future! Without His vision, we won't have hope. He says, if you are oppressed (beat down and worn out) you are to come to Him and He will set you free, because His yoke is easy, and His burden is light. His Word says so! He doesn't go back on His Word.

- 2 Corinthians 3:17 – *"Now the Lord is the Spirit; and where the Spirit of the Lord is, there is liberty."*

Is the Spirit of the Lord in you? If you have made Jesus your Lord, the answer is an emphatic yes! So that means, according to these verses, you are free! That means you have the upper hand on the enemy. So, when the enemy comes to bring us back into bondage, we can confidently say, if we have repented, closed all these doors, and submitted to God, we can confidently resist the devil and the Word of God tells us he must flee from us (James 4:7). We are free from his condemnation. Take a stand! Don't allow the enemy to rob you of your freedom and put you in bondage.

- Galatians 5:1 – *"Stand fast therefore in the liberty by which Christ has made us free, and do not be entangled again with a yoke of bondage."*

Trust in Him!

- Psalm 71:1 – *"In You, O Lord, I put my trust; Let*

me never be put to shame."

- Shame means confusion here.

When we trust in God, we will be free from confusion. When we know who has our back in life, we have peace and confidence! This is what God longs for--He wants us to be free of confusion.

Dwell in Him, which means to take residence in Him, or to move in with Him.

- Psalm 27:4 & 5 – *"One thing I have desired of the Lord, that will I seek: That I may dwell in the house of the Lord All the days of my life, To behold the beauty of the Lord, And to inquire in His temple. For in the time of trouble He shall hide me in His pavilion; In the secret place of His tabernacle, He shall hide me; He shall set me high upon a rock."*

- Let Him be in every part of your life. He says in times of trouble (confusion) He will hide you! How does that sound? It sounds really good to me!

- Psalm 91:1 – *"He who dwells in the secret place of the Most High Shall abide under the shadow of the Almighty."*

He says in this verse we will be under His shadow. Sounds like a great place to be. Do you think there is confusion in God's shadow? A BIG NEGATIVE, NADA, NOT!

A CALL TO CLARITY

Pray!

- Nehemiah 4:8 & 9 – *"...and all of them conspired together to come and attack Jerusalem and create confusion. Nevertheless, we made our prayer to our God, and because of them we set a watch against them day and night."*

The enemy conspires to bring confusion against us, so we cannot accomplish the task that God has for us. Prayer breaks the plan of the enemy and it will bring clarity to our situations. Pray without ceasing and see victory. Break the back of confusion in your life.

CONFUSION BREAKER

In Nehemiah Chapter Seven, the people were coming back from captivity in Babylon (confusion). When we are in a place for a long time, that environment rubs off on us. Think about your own upbringing. You learned good and bad from the environment in which you were brought up. If you have been struggling for a long time with confusion, you need some reprogramming. The way you do that is with the Word of God.

Here is a great story in Nehemiah 8: 1-4,12.

- Nehemiah 8:1: *"Now all the people gathered together as one man in the open square that was in front of the Water Gate; and they told Ezra the scribe to bring the Book of the Law of Moses, which the Lord had commanded Israel. So Ezra the priest brought the Law before the assembly of men and women and all who could hear with understanding on the first day of the seventh month. Then he read from it in the open square that was in front of the Water Gate from morning until midday, before the men and women and those who could understand; and the ears of all the people were attentive to the Book of the Law. So Ezra (help) the scribe stood on a platform of wood which they had made for the purpose; and beside him, at his right hand, stood Mattithiah (gift), Shema (sound), Anaiah, Urijah (flame) Hilkiah (My portion), and Maaseiah (work); and at his left hand Pedaiah (ransomed), Mishael, Malchijah (king), Hashum, Hashbadana, Zechariah, and Meshullam."*

- *"And all the people went their way to eat and drink, to send portions and rejoice greatly, because they understood the words that were declared to them" (verse 12).*

Ezra read the Word of God to break off confusion! Ezra, whose name means "help" (which isn't a coincidence), knew what the people needed to break the confusion was the Word of God. Just think of what the people were like when they got back from Babylon. They were a confused mess—or in today's vernacular, "dysfunctional." The Word frees us! Ezra also surrounded himself with good people to help minister the Word. This is great picture of how ministry should work. The names of the people who surrounded Ezra meant the following: Help, Gift, Flame, Sound, My Portion, Ransomed, Work, and King.

Here is a word God pressed on my heart from this passage to encourage us:

For as the enemy has brought confusion to bring disorder to your life but the Lord has brought His Help through His Word to break the bondage of confusion. It is a Gift from Him and is like a Flame that is impossible to extinguish. Speak the Word out loud with a Sound that brings trembling to the enemy's camp! You are the Lord's Portion. You are part of a royal army. Settle only for the best. You have been Ransomed by the King of Kings and the Lord of Lords, Jesus Christ. You have called to do the Work of the King. To be Kingdom-minded and to walk out the Great Commission, in total freedom!

FINAL REMINDERS

- Hebrews 13:8
  "Jesus Christ is the same yesterday, today, and forever."

In other words, if God can pull someone out of a confused state yesterday, He can do it today!

Isaiah 61:7 – *"Instead of your shame you shall have* double *honor, And instead of confusion they shall rejoice in their portion. Therefore, in their land they shall* *possess double; Everlasting joy shall be theirs."*

God wants to give us honor instead of shame, no more confusion. Double blessings and everlasting joy are meant to be ours!

- Let's repent if we need to and close the door.

- Jesus Christ is the answer. Seek Him first!

- Dive into His Word and be set free!

- Speak His Word over yourself!

- Operate out of the Mind of Christ, not the carnal mind!

- Confusion can go now!

- Walk in victory! Jesus won this battle 2000 years ago!

Here is a prayer we can pray to break out of the bondage of confusion.

Jesus, I repent and renounce all of the following: pride, idol worship, rebellion, a religious spirit, unrepentance, disobedience, envy, jealousy, self-seeking, perversion, shame, treason/lying that has been part of my life and I ask for your forgiveness. Now that these things are under the Blood of Jesus Christ, the enemy now no longer has legal ground, so in the Name of Jesus I command all confusion to leave me now and I forbid it to return. Lord, fill me with Your clarity. Help me operate out of the mind of Christ from this day forth. Amen. Thank You, Lord Jesus!

SOMETHING TO THINK ABOUT.

Read the story of Ezra in Nehemiah 8 and how the Word set the people free from confusion.

How does the Word set you free?

What verses resonate with you? Write them down!

Are there any open doors that you need to deal with? If so, please do so you can be free.

Allow God to fill you with His truth and deliver you from the enemy's oppression.

If you haven't made Jesus Christ your Lord and Savior, we would love to pray with you. Please contact Releasing Life Ministries at: Releasinglifeministries@gmail.com

For teaching/preaching engagements contact releasinglifeministries@gmail.com.

About the Author

Jeff Shattell, the youngest of seven children, was born and raised in Syracuse New York. Growing up, Jeff's family attended church every Sunday, but it wasn't until his mid 30's that he received Jesus as Lord and Savior. It's been a treasure hunt ever since. As Jeff has dug into the Word and found those nuggets of truth and wisdom, it's not surprising that he penned a book on confusion. His desire is to see God's people whole and walking out their destiny is what drives his studying, writing, speaking, and even the revelation he receives from the Lord. Jeff's ministry and educational experience with various churches, The Healing Rooms, Transformation Syracuse, Wagner Leadership Institute, and others has also contributed to his life and writings. With his free time, Jeff enjoys his family and following sports, although there is nothing, he enjoys more than a conversation about the Lord. Jeff and his wife Kim recently relocated to Virginia Beach, Virginia.

You can connect with Jeff at:

https://www.facebook.com/pages/category/
Religious-Organization/Releasing-Life-Ministries-102385044498128/
or ReleasingLife.com
Releasinglifeministries@gmail.com